GraphicScience Biographies

MARIE CURIE AND RADIOACTIVITY

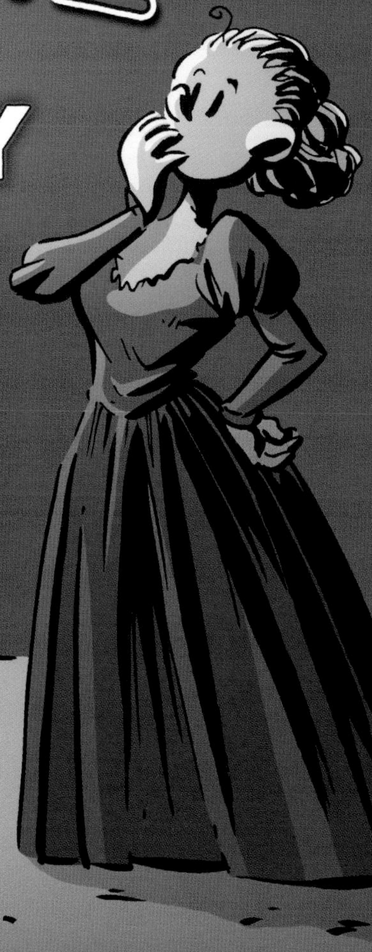

JORDI BAYARRI

GRAPHIC UNIVERSE™ • MINNEAPOLIS

Story and art by Jordi Bayarri
Coloring by Dani Seijas
Historical and scientific consultation by Dr. Tayra M. C. Lanuza-Navarro, PhD in History of Science
Translation by Patricia Ibars and John Wright

First American edition published in 2020 by Graphic Universe™

Graphic Universe™
An imprint of Lerner Publishing Group, Inc.
241 First Avenue North
Minneapolis, MN 55401 USA

For reading levels and more information, look up this title at www.lernerbooks.com.

Image credit: Bettmann/Getty Images, p. 37

Main body text set in CCDaveGibbonsLower.
Typeface provided by OpenType.

Library of Congress Cataloging-in-Publication Data

Names: Bayarri, Jordi, 1972- author, illustrator.
Title: Marie Curie and radiation / Jordi Bayarri.
Description: Minneapolis : Graphic Universe, [2020] I Series: Graphic science biographies I "Graphic Universe is a trademark of Lerner Publishing Group, Inc." I Audience: Ages 10-14. I Audience: Grades 7 to 8. I Includes bibliographical references and index.
Identifiers: LCCN 2019006971 I ISBN 9781541578210 (lb : alk. paper)
Subjects: LCSH: Curie, Marie, 1867-1934—Comic books, strips, etc. I Curie, Marie, 1867-1934—Juvenile literature. I Radioactivity—History—Comic books, strips, etc. I Radioactivity—History—Juvenile literature. I Women chemists—France—Biography—Comic books, strips, etc. I Women chemists—France—Biography—Juvenile literature. I Women Nobel Prize winners—Biography—Comic books, strips, etc. I Women Nobel Prize winners—Biography—Juvenile literature. I Discoveries in science—Comic books, strips, etc. I Discoveries in science—Juvenile literature.
Classification: LCC QD22.C8 B39 2020 I DDC 540.92 [B]—dc23

LC record available at https://lccn.loc.gov/2019006971

Manufactured in the United States of America
1-46926-47806-5/21/2019

CONTENTS

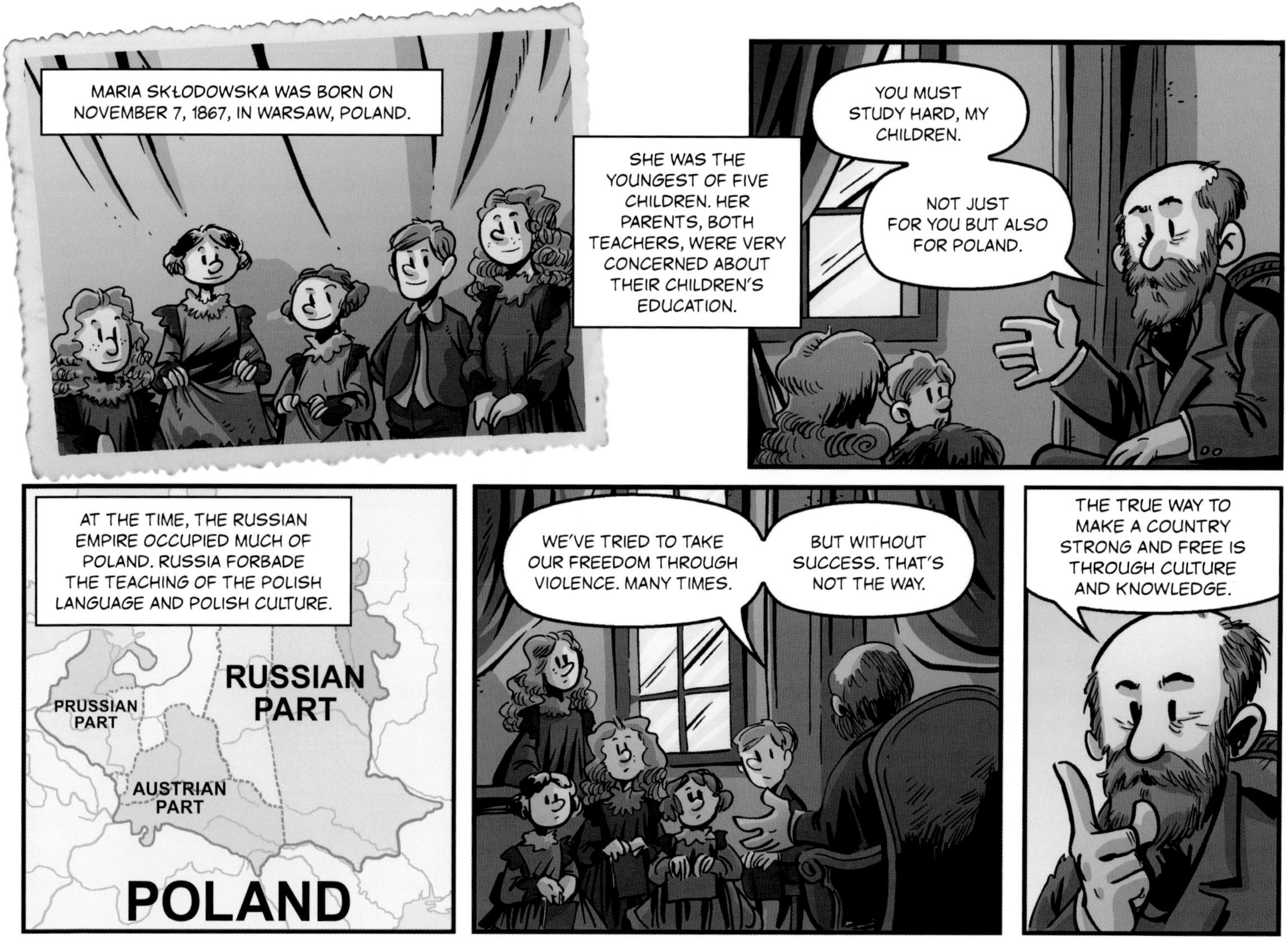
MARIA SKŁODOWSKA WAS BORN ON NOVEMBER 7, 1867, IN WARSAW, POLAND.
SHE WAS THE YOUNGEST OF FIVE CHILDREN. HER PARENTS, BOTH TEACHERS, WERE VERY CONCERNED ABOUT THEIR CHILDREN'S EDUCATION.
YOU MUST STUDY HARD, MY CHILDREN.
NOT JUST FOR YOU BUT ALSO FOR POLAND.
AT THE TIME, THE RUSSIAN EMPIRE OCCUPIED MUCH OF POLAND. RUSSIA FORBADE THE TEACHING OF THE POLISH LANGUAGE AND POLISH CULTURE.
RUSSIAN PART
PRUSSIAN PART
AUSTRIAN PART
POLAND
WE'VE TRIED TO TAKE OUR FREEDOM THROUGH VIOLENCE. MANY TIMES.
BUT WITHOUT SUCCESS. THAT'S NOT THE WAY.
THE TRUE WAY TO MAKE A COUNTRY STRONG AND FREE IS THROUGH CULTURE AND KNOWLEDGE.

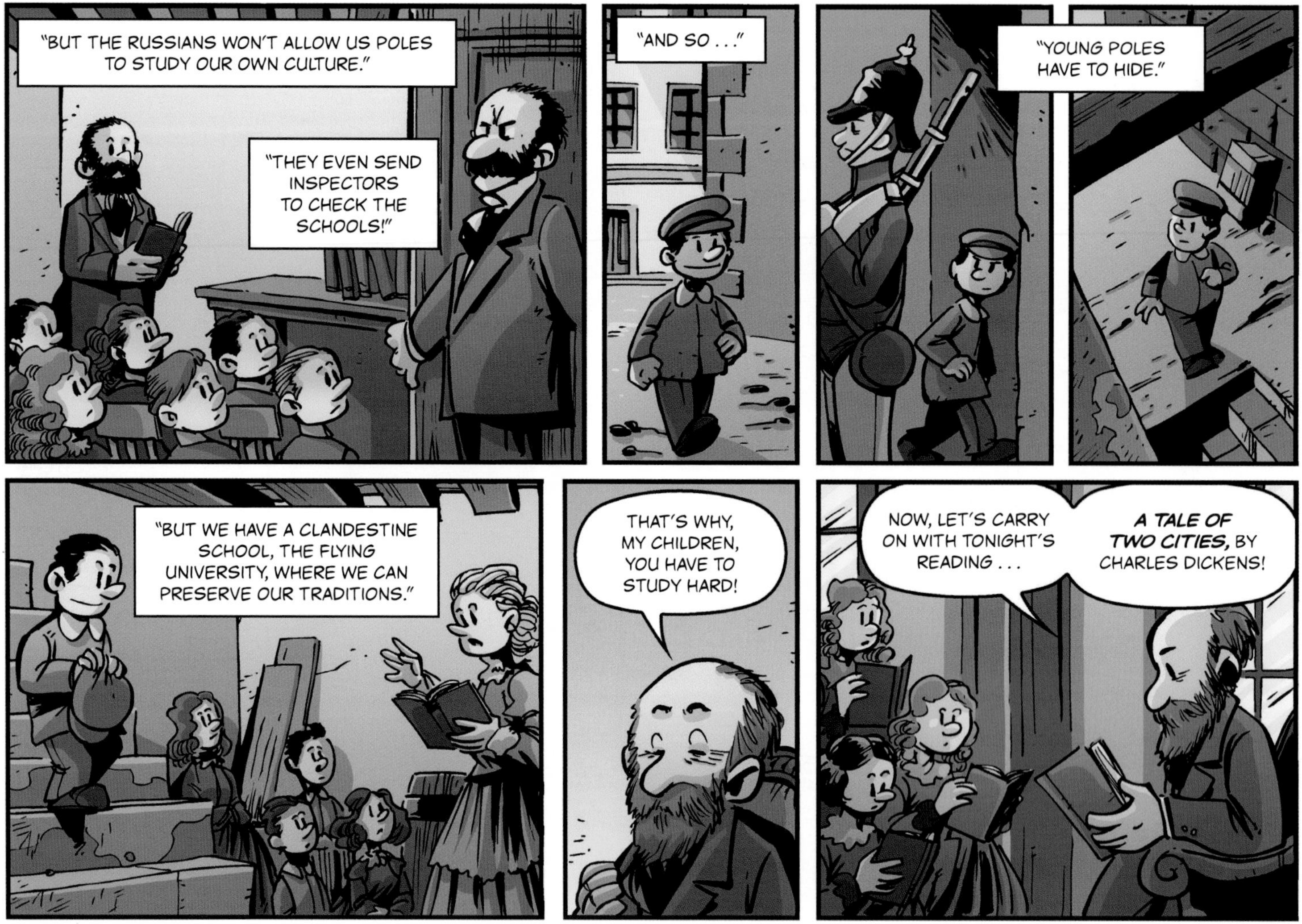
"BUT THE RUSSIANS WON'T ALLOW US POLES TO STUDY OUR OWN CULTURE."
"THEY EVEN SEND INSPECTORS TO CHECK THE SCHOOLS!"
"AND SO . . ."
"YOUNG POLES HAVE TO HIDE."
"BUT WE HAVE A CLANDESTINE SCHOOL, THE FLYING UNIVERSITY, WHERE WE CAN PRESERVE OUR TRADITIONS."
THAT'S WHY, MY CHILDREN, YOU HAVE TO STUDY HARD!
NOW, LET'S CARRY ON WITH TONIGHT'S READING . . .
A TALE OF TWO CITIES, BY CHARLES DICKENS!

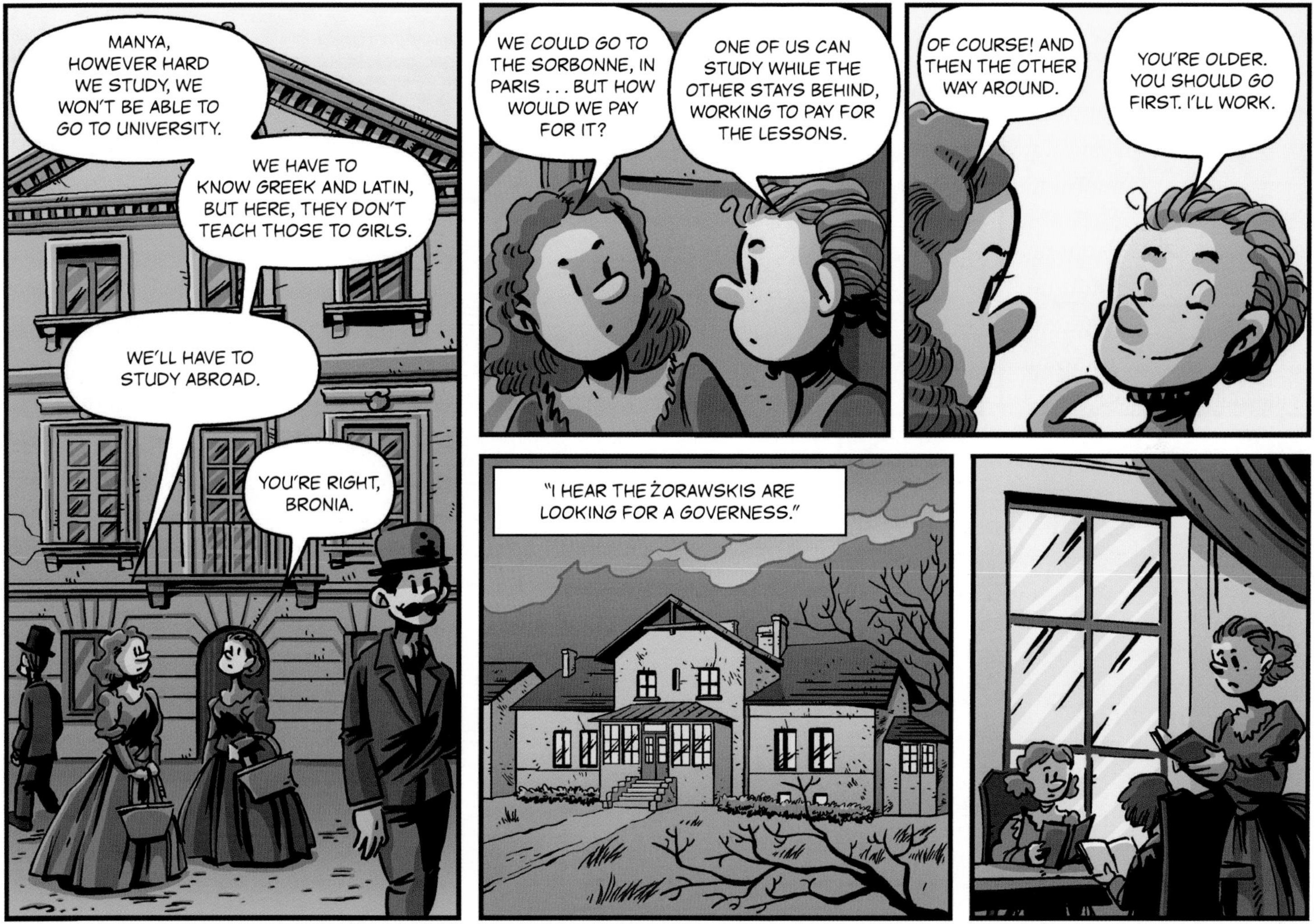
MANYA, HOWEVER HARD WE STUDY, WE WON'T BE ABLE TO GO TO UNIVERSITY.
WE HAVE TO KNOW GREEK AND LATIN, BUT HERE, THEY DON'T TEACH THOSE TO GIRLS.
WE'LL HAVE TO STUDY ABROAD.
YOU'RE RIGHT, BRONIA.
WE COULD GO TO THE SORBONNE, IN PARIS . . . BUT HOW WOULD WE PAY FOR IT?
ONE OF US CAN STUDY WHILE THE OTHER STAYS BEHIND, WORKING TO PAY FOR THE LESSONS.
OF COURSE! AND THEN THE OTHER WAY AROUND.
YOU'RE OLDER. YOU SHOULD GO FIRST. I'LL WORK.
"I HEAR THE ŻORAWSKIS ARE LOOKING FOR A GOVERNESS."

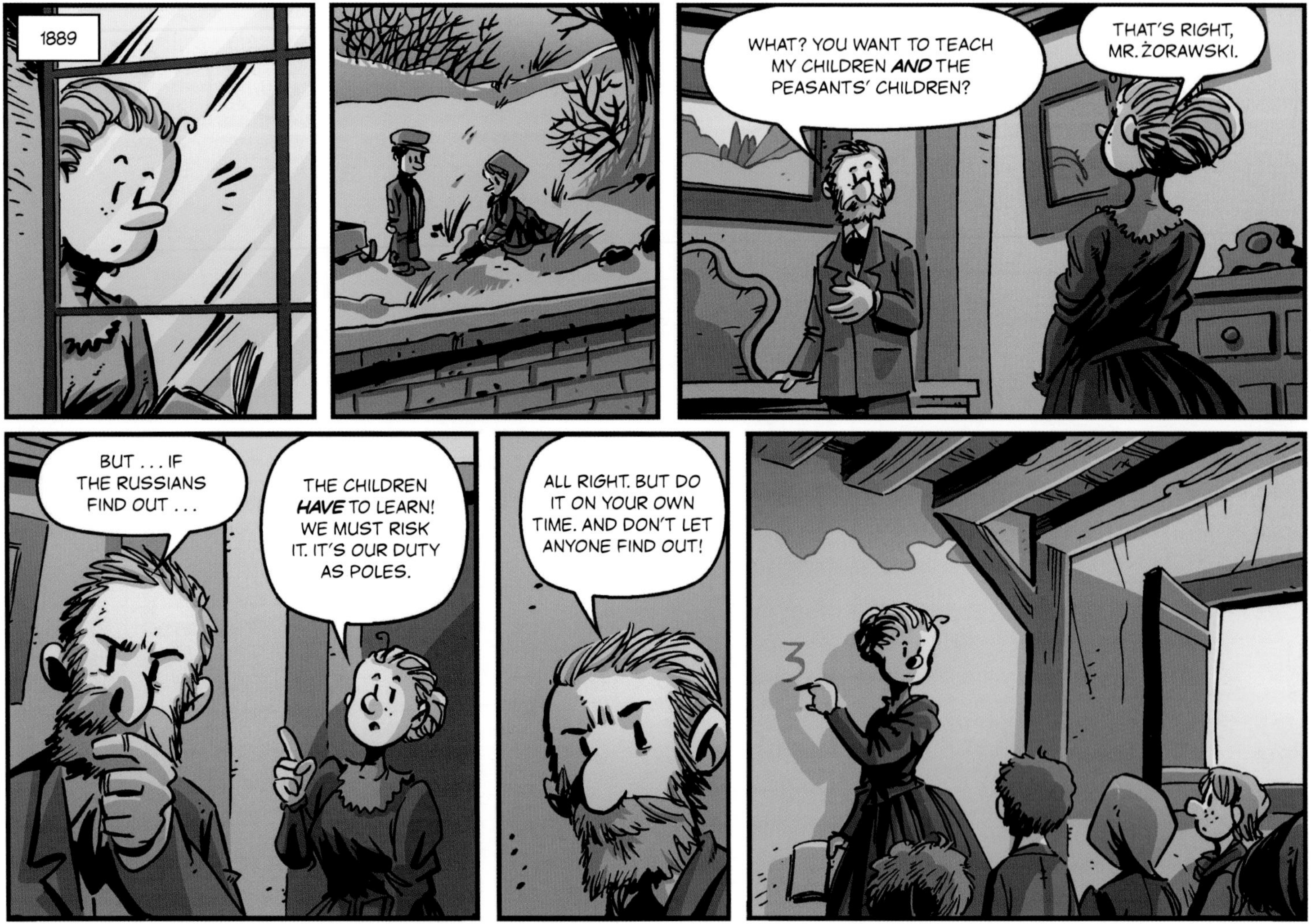
1889
WHAT? YOU WANT TO TEACH MY CHILDREN AND THE PEASANTS' CHILDREN?
THAT'S RIGHT, MR. ŻORAWSKI.
BUT . . . IF THE RUSSIANS FIND OUT . . .
THE CHILDREN HAVE TO LEARN! WE MUST RISK IT. IT'S OUR DUTY AS POLES.
ALL RIGHT. BUT DO IT ON YOUR OWN TIME. AND DON'T LET ANYONE FIND OUT!
3

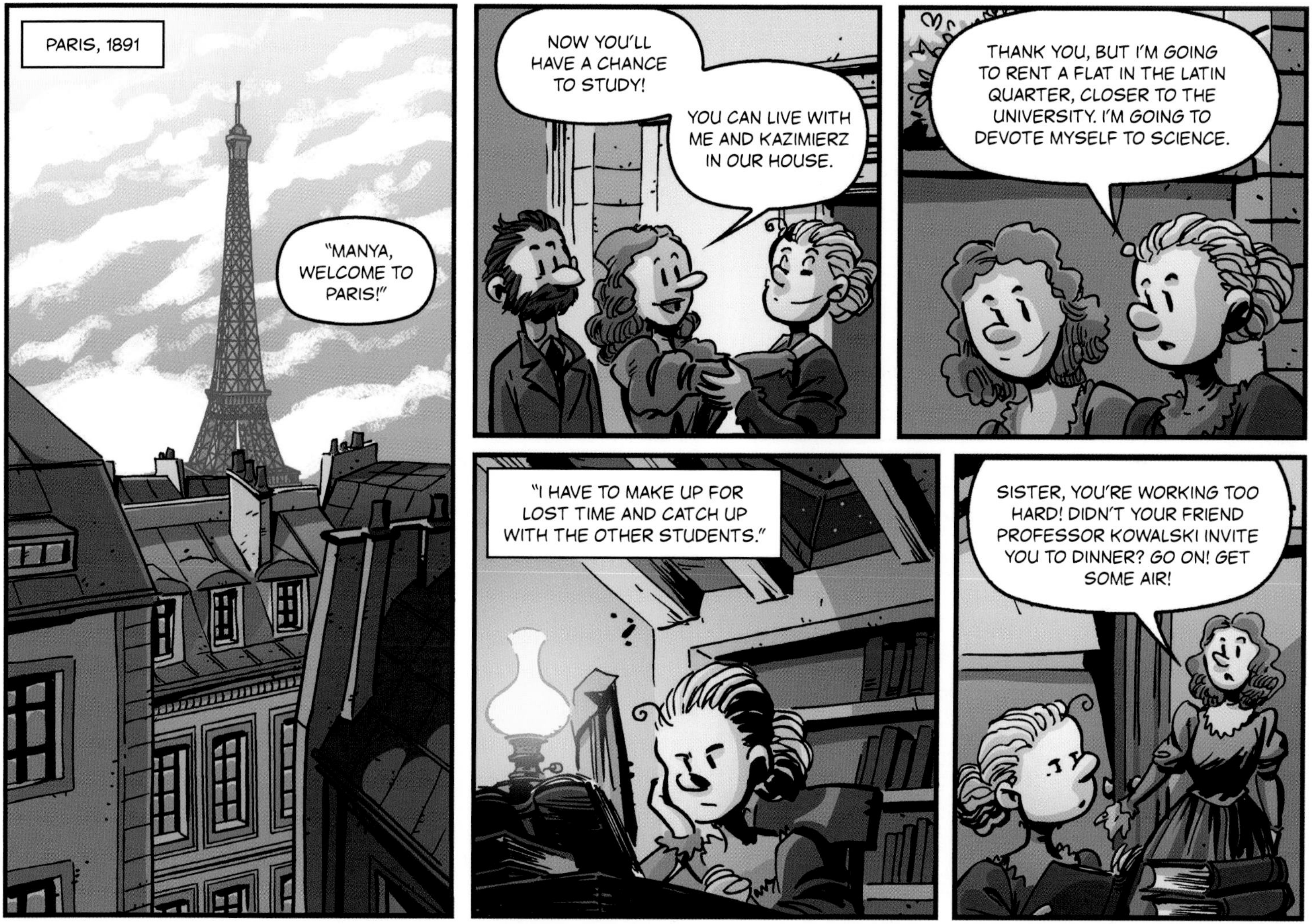
PARIS, 1891
"MANYA, WELCOME TO PARIS!"
NOW YOU'LL HAVE A CHANCE TO STUDY!
YOU CAN LIVE WITH ME AND KAZIMIERZ IN OUR HOUSE.
THANK YOU, BUT I'M GOING TO RENT A FLAT IN THE LATIN QUARTER, CLOSER TO THE UNIVERSITY. I'M GOING TO DEVOTE MYSELF TO SCIENCE.
"I HAVE TO MAKE UP FOR LOST TIME AND CATCH UP WITH THE OTHER STUDENTS."
SISTER, YOU'RE WORKING TOO HARD! DIDN'T YOUR FRIEND PROFESSOR KOWALSKI INVITE YOU TO DINNER? GO ON! GET SOME AIR!

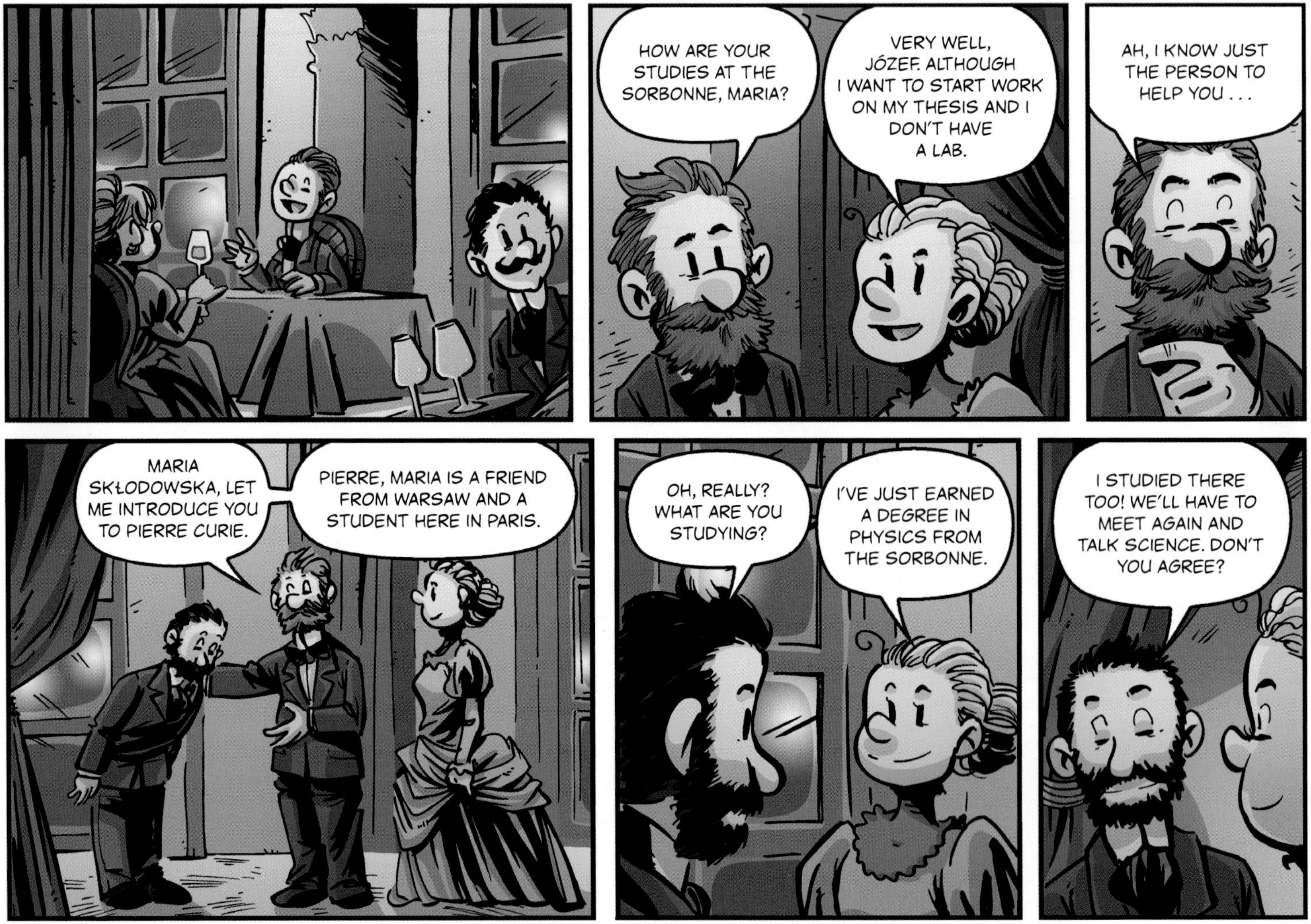
HOW ARE YOUR STUDIES AT THE SORBONNE, MARIA?
VERY WELL, JÓZEF. ALTHOUGH I WANT TO START WORK ON MY THESIS AND I DON'T HAVE A LAB.
AH, I KNOW JUST THE PERSON TO HELP YOU . . .
MARIA SKŁODOWSKA, LET ME INTRODUCE YOU TO PIERRE CURIE.
PIERRE, MARIA IS A FRIEND FROM WARSAW AND A STUDENT HERE IN PARIS.
OH, REALLY? WHAT ARE YOU STUDYING?
I'VE JUST EARNED A DEGREE IN PHYSICS FROM THE SORBONNE.
I STUDIED THERE TOO! WE'LL HAVE TO MEET AGAIN AND TALK SCIENCE. DON'T YOU AGREE?

SO WHAT'S YOUR FIELD OF STUDY, MR. CURIE?

WELL, MY FATHER WAS A DOCTOR, SO AT HOME WE HAD A KEEN INTEREST IN SCIENCE. AND LIKE YOU, I STUDIED PHYSICS AT THE SORBONNE.

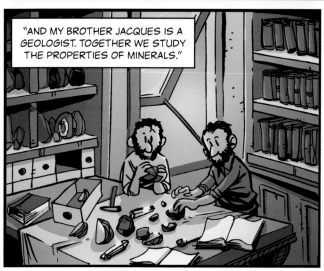

"AND MY BROTHER JACQUES IS A GEOLOGIST. TOGETHER WE STUDY THE PROPERTIES OF MINERALS."

WE'VE EVEN FOUND THAT SOME MINERALS GENERATE ELECTRICITY IF WE APPLY PRESSURE. WE CALL IT *PIEZOELECTRICITY.*

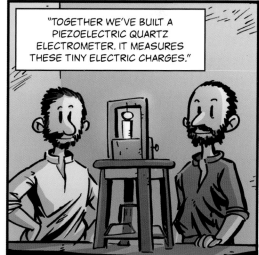

"TOGETHER WE'VE BUILT A PIEZOELECTRIC QUARTZ ELECTROMETER. IT MEASURES THESE TINY ELECTRIC CHARGES."

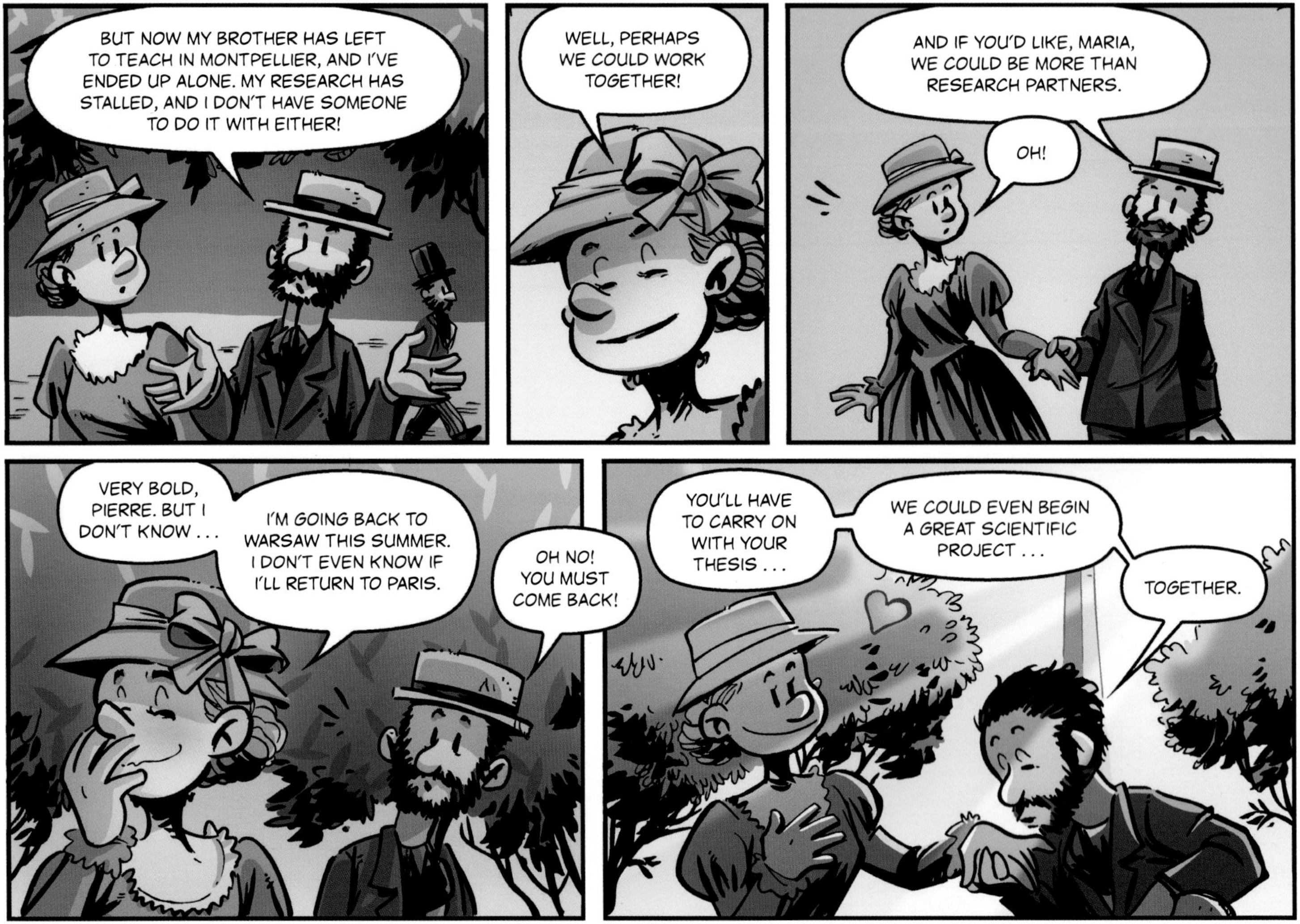
BUT NOW MY BROTHER HAS LEFT TO TEACH IN MONTPELLIER, AND I'VE ENDED UP ALONE. MY RESEARCH HAS STALLED, AND I DON'T HAVE SOMEONE TO DO IT WITH EITHER!
WELL, PERHAPS WE COULD WORK TOGETHER!
AND IF YOU'D LIKE, MARIA, WE COULD BE MORE THAN RESEARCH PARTNERS.
OH!
VERY BOLD, PIERRE. BUT I DON'T KNOW . . .
I'M GOING BACK TO WARSAW THIS SUMMER. I DON'T EVEN KNOW IF I'LL RETURN TO PARIS.
OH NO! YOU MUST COME BACK!
YOU'LL HAVE TO CARRY ON WITH YOUR THESIS . . .
WE COULD EVEN BEGIN A GREAT SCIENTIFIC PROJECT . . .
TOGETHER.

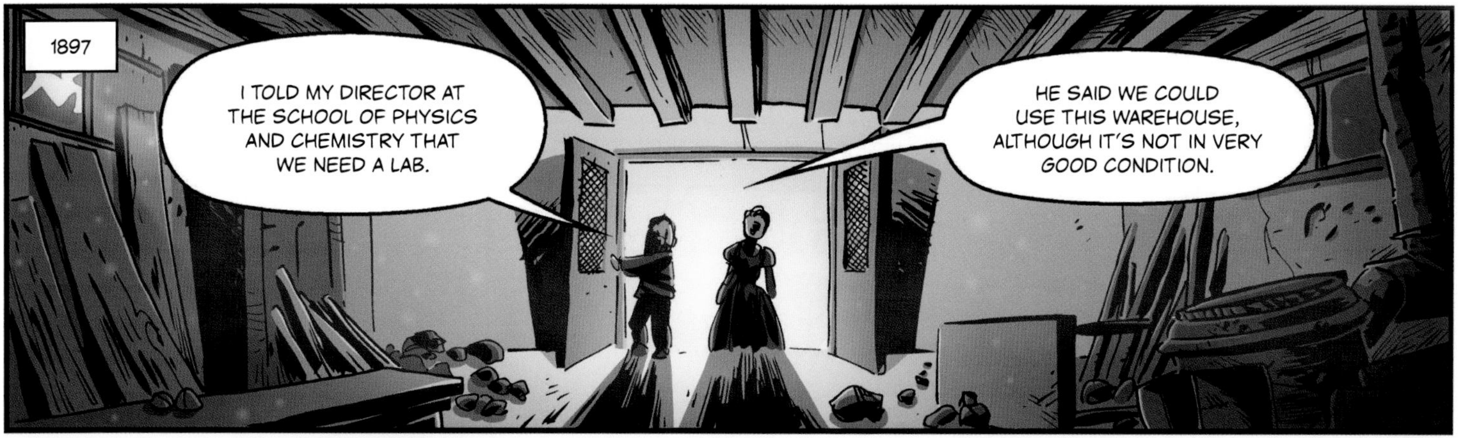
1897
I TOLD MY DIRECTOR AT THE SCHOOL OF PHYSICS AND CHEMISTRY THAT WE NEED A LAB.
HE SAID WE COULD USE THIS WAREHOUSE, ALTHOUGH IT'S NOT IN VERY GOOD CONDITION.

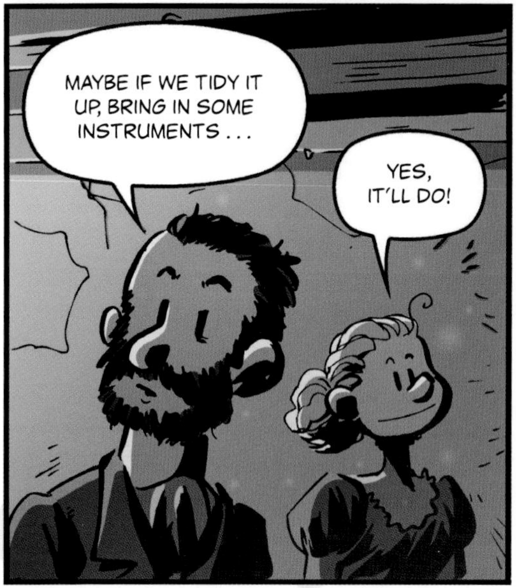
MAYBE IF WE TIDY IT UP, BRING IN SOME INSTRUMENTS . . .
YES, IT'LL DO!

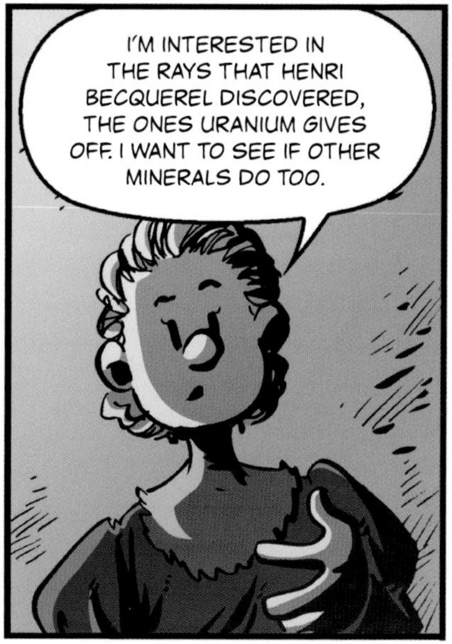
I'M INTERESTED IN THE RAYS THAT HENRI BECQUEREL DISCOVERED, THE ONES URANIUM GIVES OFF. I WANT TO SEE IF OTHER MINERALS DO TOO.

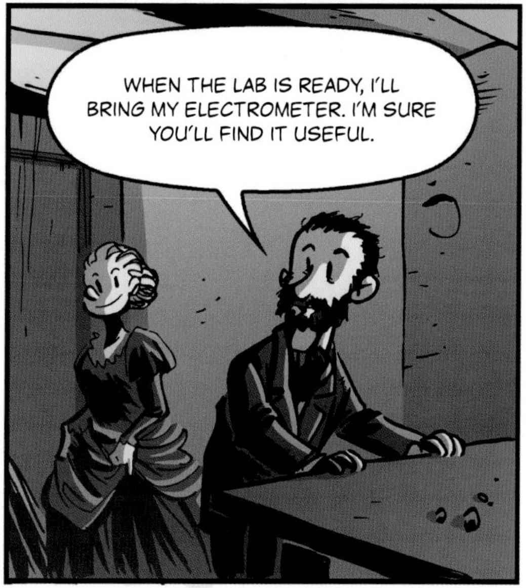
WHEN THE LAB IS READY, I'LL BRING MY ELECTROMETER. I'M SURE YOU'LL FIND IT USEFUL.

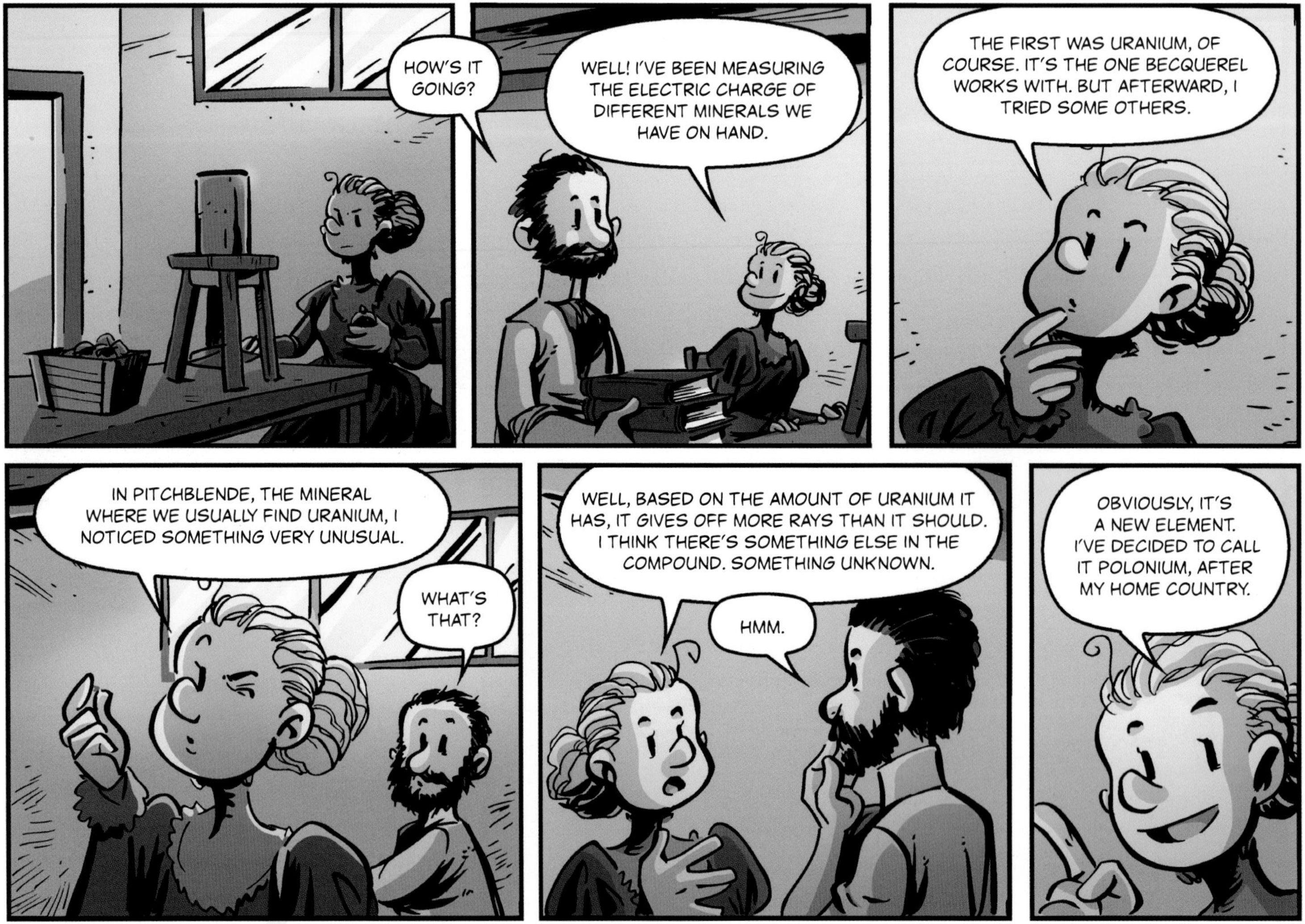
HOW'S IT GOING?
WELL! I'VE BEEN MEASURING THE ELECTRIC CHARGE OF DIFFERENT MINERALS WE HAVE ON HAND.
THE FIRST WAS URANIUM, OF COURSE. IT'S THE ONE BECQUEREL WORKS WITH. BUT AFTERWARD, I TRIED SOME OTHERS.
IN PITCHBLENDE, THE MINERAL WHERE WE USUALLY FIND URANIUM, I NOTICED SOMETHING VERY UNUSUAL.
WHAT'S THAT?
WELL, BASED ON THE AMOUNT OF URANIUM IT HAS, IT GIVES OFF MORE RAYS THAN IT SHOULD. I THINK THERE'S SOMETHING ELSE IN THE COMPOUND. SOMETHING UNKNOWN.
HMM.
OBVIOUSLY, IT'S A NEW ELEMENT. I'VE DECIDED TO CALL IT POLONIUM, AFTER MY HOME COUNTRY.

1898

SEE? FROM TIME TO TIME, YOU SHOULD STOP TO EAT AND REST.

I KNOW. BUT I'M SO ABSORBED IN MY WORK!

I'VE DISCOVERED YET ANOTHER ELEMENT WITHIN PITCHBLENDE. IT GIVES OFF EVEN MORE RAYS THAN THE OTHERS . . .

I THINK I'LL CALL IT RADIUM, WHICH MEANS "*RAY*" IN LATIN. ITS LEVEL OF EMISSIONS IS HUGE! SO MANY RAYS . . . IT'S LIKE A KIND OF . . .

RADIOACTIVITY.

YES, THAT'S IT.

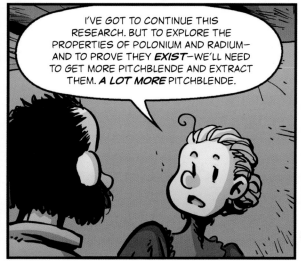

I'VE GOT TO CONTINUE THIS RESEARCH. BUT TO EXPLORE THE PROPERTIES OF POLONIUM AND RADIUM—AND TO PROVE THEY *EXIST*—WE'LL NEED TO GET MORE PITCHBLENDE AND EXTRACT THEM. *A LOT MORE* PITCHBLENDE.

YES, YOU'RE RIGHT. HMM. I KNOW A GEOLOGIST AT THE UNIVERSITY OF VIENNA . . . HE MIGHT BE ABLE TO HELP US . . .

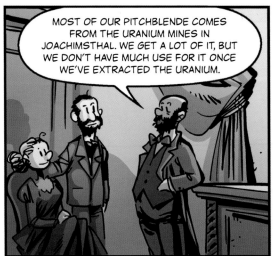

MOST OF OUR PITCHBLENDE COMES FROM THE URANIUM MINES IN JOACHIMSTHAL. WE GET A LOT OF IT, BUT WE DON'T HAVE MUCH USE FOR IT ONCE WE'VE EXTRACTED THE URANIUM.

WELL, THAT'S PERFECT FOR US. WITHOUT URANIUM IN THE MINERAL, IT'S EASIER TO DETECT AND REFINE THE NEW ELEMENTS.

THEN EVERYBODY WINS! WE GET RID OF OUR LEFTOVER PITCHBLENDE, AND YOU GET MINERALS FOR YOUR RESEARCH . . .

FOR A REASONABLE PRICE, OF COURSE.

MR. CURIE, YOUR MINERALS ARE HERE. WHERE SHOULD WE PUT THEM?

HERE IS FINE.

BUT . . .

ALL OF THEM?

AND THEY SAY THEY'RE GOING TO SEND MORE! MMFF!

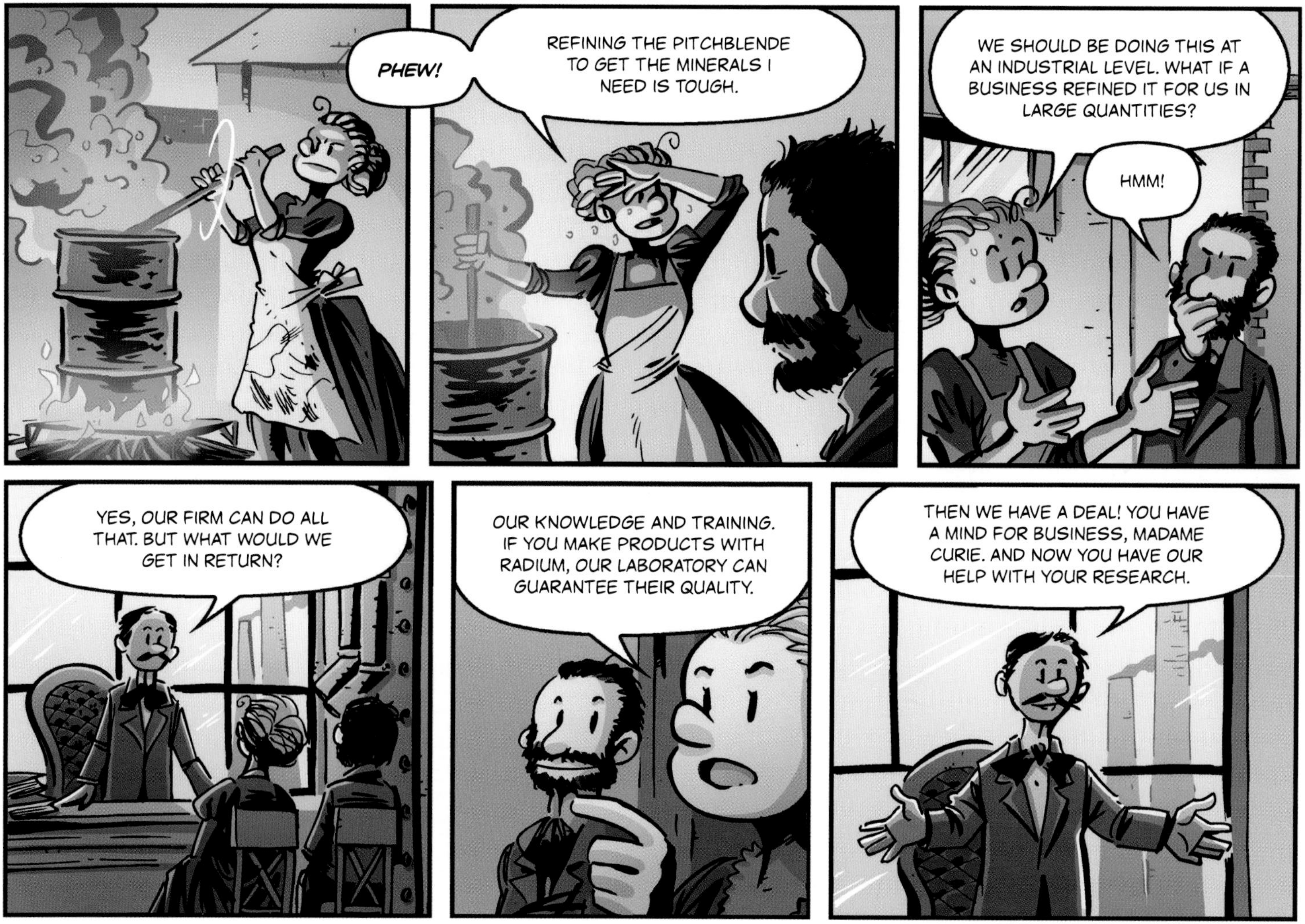
PHEW!
REFINING THE PITCHBLENDE TO GET THE MINERALS I NEED IS TOUGH.
WE SHOULD BE DOING THIS AT AN INDUSTRIAL LEVEL. WHAT IF A BUSINESS REFINED IT FOR US IN LARGE QUANTITIES?
HMM!
YES, OUR FIRM CAN DO ALL THAT. BUT WHAT WOULD WE GET IN RETURN?
OUR KNOWLEDGE AND TRAINING. IF YOU MAKE PRODUCTS WITH RADIUM, OUR LABORATORY CAN GUARANTEE THEIR QUALITY.
THEN WE HAVE A DEAL! YOU HAVE A MIND FOR BUSINESS, MADAME CURIE. AND NOW YOU HAVE OUR HELP WITH YOUR RESEARCH.

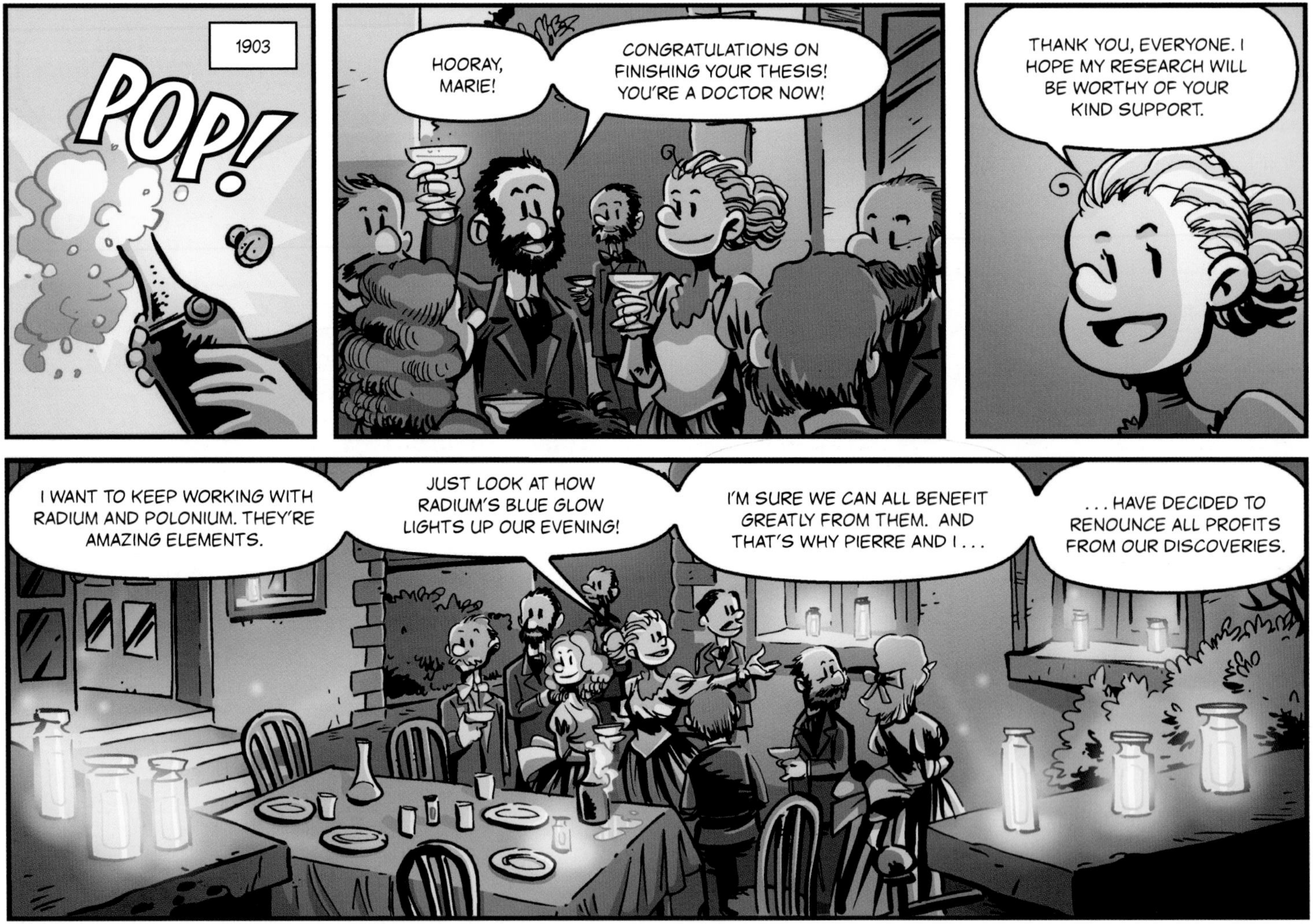
1903
POP!
HOORAY, MARIE!
CONGRATULATIONS ON FINISHING YOUR THESIS! YOU'RE A DOCTOR NOW!
THANK YOU, EVERYONE. I HOPE MY RESEARCH WILL BE WORTHY OF YOUR KIND SUPPORT.
I WANT TO KEEP WORKING WITH RADIUM AND POLONIUM. THEY'RE AMAZING ELEMENTS.
JUST LOOK AT HOW RADIUM'S BLUE GLOW LIGHTS UP OUR EVENING!
I'M SURE WE CAN ALL BENEFIT GREATLY FROM THEM. AND THAT'S WHY PIERRE AND I . . .
. . . HAVE DECIDED TO RENOUNCE ALL PROFITS FROM OUR DISCOVERIES.

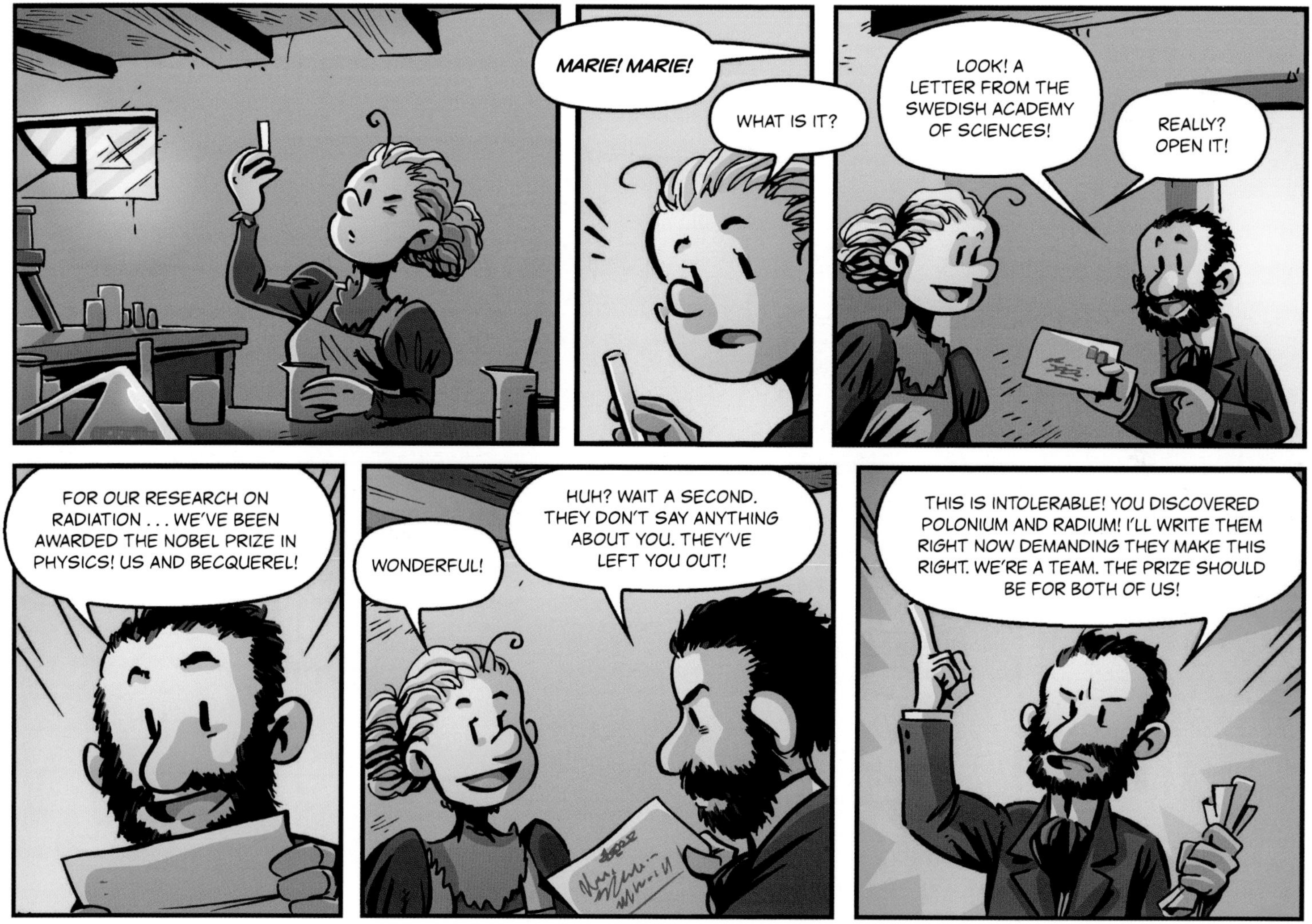
MARIE! MARIE!
WHAT IS IT?
LOOK! A LETTER FROM THE SWEDISH ACADEMY OF SCIENCES!
REALLY? OPEN IT!
FOR OUR RESEARCH ON RADIATION . . . WE'VE BEEN AWARDED THE NOBEL PRIZE IN PHYSICS! US AND BECQUEREL!
WONDERFUL!
HUH? WAIT A SECOND. THEY DON'T SAY ANYTHING ABOUT YOU. THEY'VE LEFT YOU OUT!
THIS IS INTOLERABLE! YOU DISCOVERED POLONIUM AND RADIUM! I'LL WRITE THEM RIGHT NOW DEMANDING THEY MAKE THIS RIGHT. WE'RE A TEAM. THE PRIZE SHOULD BE FOR BOTH OF US!

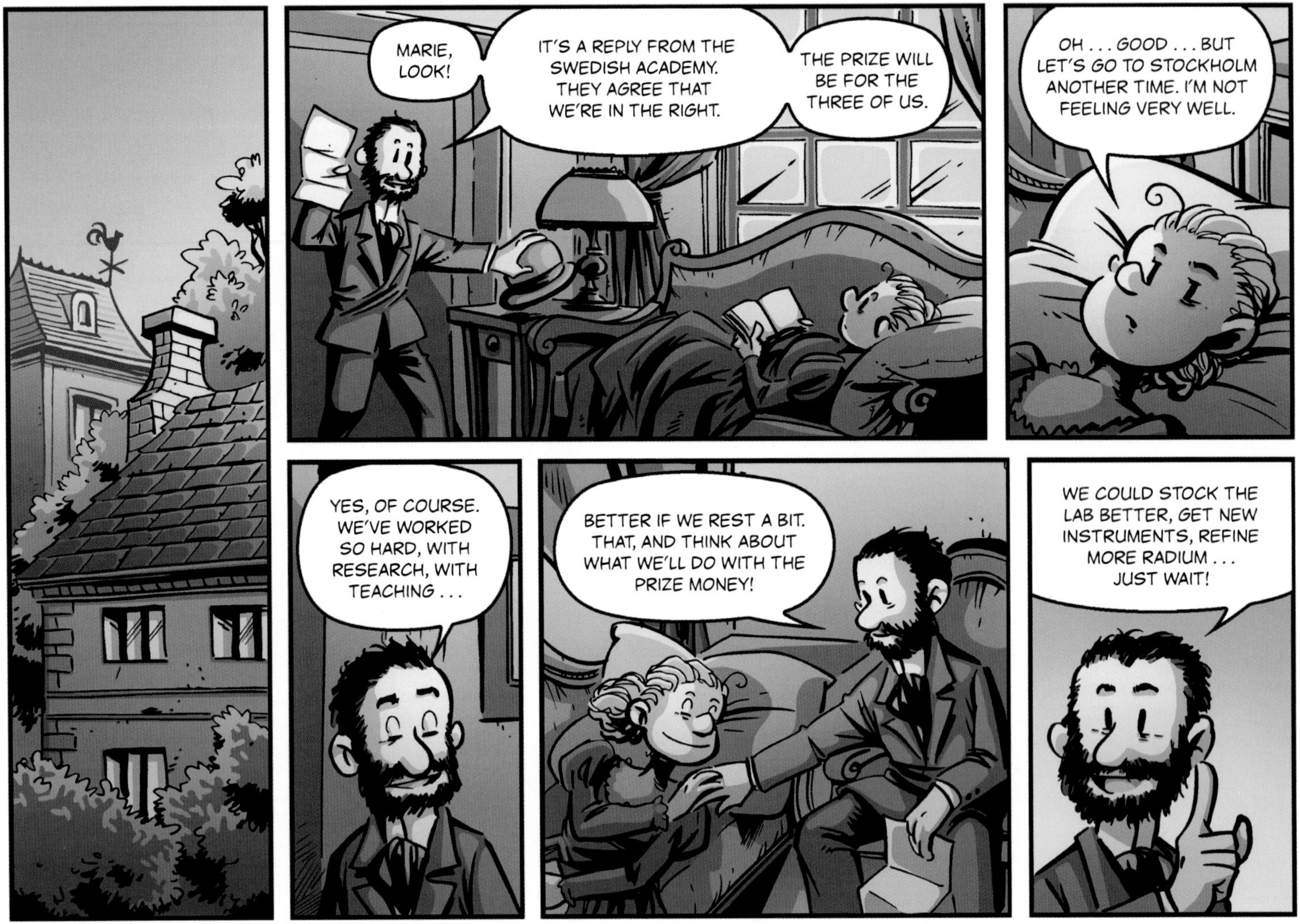
MARIE, LOOK!
IT'S A REPLY FROM THE SWEDISH ACADEMY. THEY AGREE THAT WE'RE IN THE RIGHT.
THE PRIZE WILL BE FOR THE THREE OF US.
OH . . . GOOD . . . BUT LET'S GO TO STOCKHOLM ANOTHER TIME. I'M NOT FEELING VERY WELL.
YES, OF COURSE. WE'VE WORKED SO HARD, WITH RESEARCH, WITH TEACHING . . .
BETTER IF WE REST A BIT. THAT, AND THINK ABOUT WHAT WE'LL DO WITH THE PRIZE MONEY!
WE COULD STOCK THE LAB BETTER, GET NEW INSTRUMENTS, REFINE MORE RADIUM . . . JUST WAIT!

1906

LOOK OUT!

A RUNAWAY HORSE!

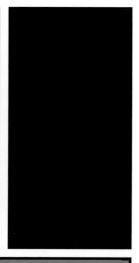

WHAT WILL YOU DO NOW, MARIE?

CONTINUE WITH MY RESEARCH, OF COURSE. MINE AND PIERRE'S!

MOTHER! A LETTER JUST ARRIVED. IT'S FROM SWEDEN.

OH, REALLY?

1911

. . . THEY'RE AWARDING ME ANOTHER NOBEL! THIS TIME IT'S FOR CHEMISTRY.

I CAN'T BELIEVE IT!

PACK YOUR BAGS, IRÈNE. WE'RE GOING TO STOCKHOLM!

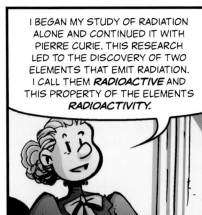

I BEGAN MY STUDY OF RADIATION ALONE AND CONTINUED IT WITH PIERRE CURIE. THIS RESEARCH LED TO THE DISCOVERY OF TWO ELEMENTS THAT EMIT RADIATION. I CALL THEM *RADIOACTIVE* AND THIS PROPERTY OF THE ELEMENTS *RADIOACTIVITY.*

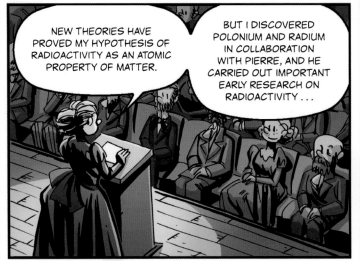

NEW THEORIES HAVE PROVED MY HYPOTHESIS OF RADIOACTIVITY AS AN ATOMIC PROPERTY OF MATTER.

BUT I DISCOVERED POLONIUM AND RADIUM IN COLLABORATION WITH PIERRE, AND HE CARRIED OUT IMPORTANT EARLY RESEARCH ON RADIOACTIVITY . . .

. . . SO THIS AWARD IS ALSO A HOMAGE TO THE MEMORY OF PIERRE CURIE.

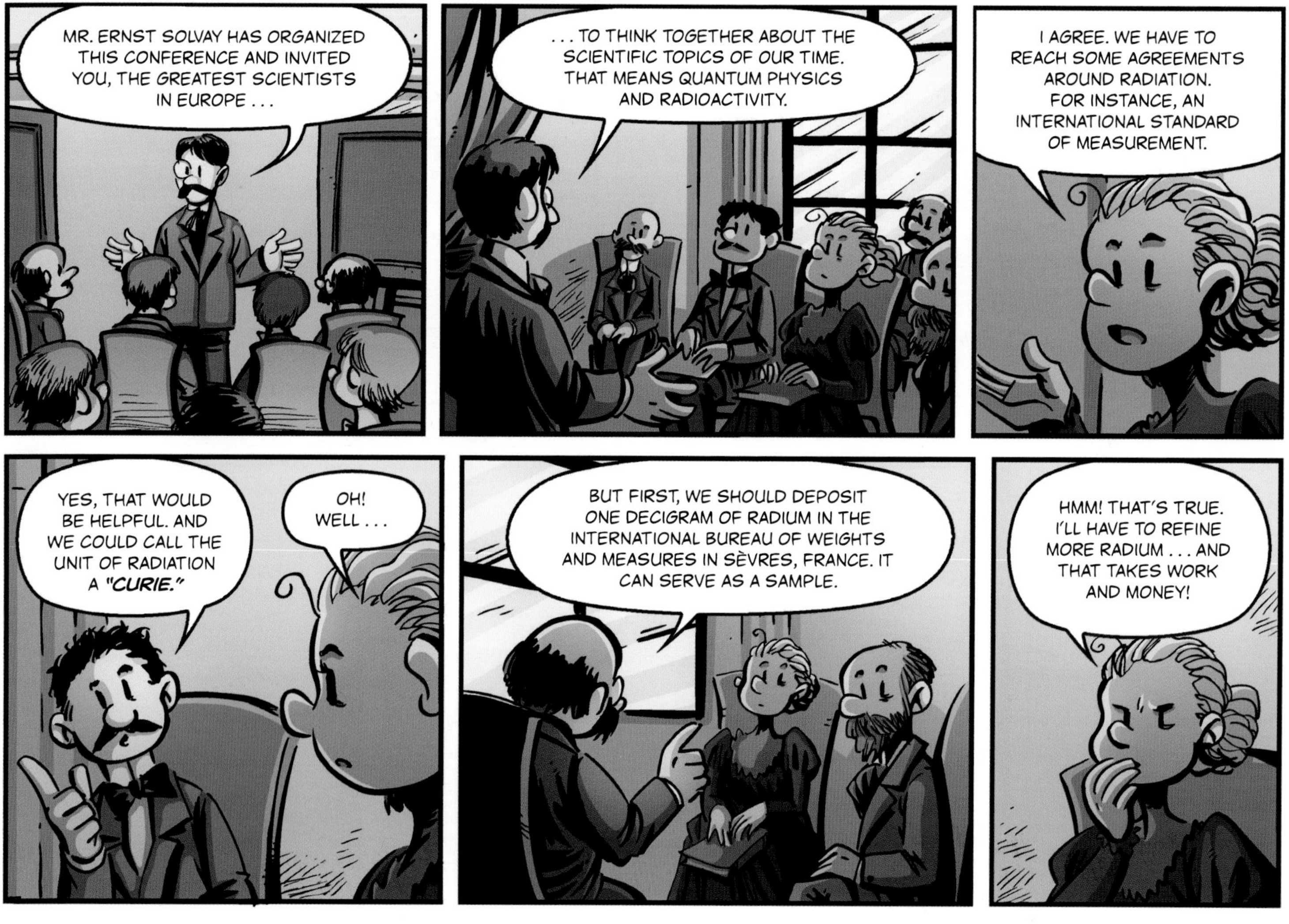
MR. ERNST SOLVAY HAS ORGANIZED THIS CONFERENCE AND INVITED YOU, THE GREATEST SCIENTISTS IN EUROPE . . .
. . . TO THINK TOGETHER ABOUT THE SCIENTIFIC TOPICS OF OUR TIME. THAT MEANS QUANTUM PHYSICS AND RADIOACTIVITY.
I AGREE. WE HAVE TO REACH SOME AGREEMENTS AROUND RADIATION. FOR INSTANCE, AN INTERNATIONAL STANDARD OF MEASUREMENT.
YES, THAT WOULD BE HELPFUL. AND WE COULD CALL THE UNIT OF RADIATION A ***"CURIE."***
OH! WELL . . .
BUT FIRST, WE SHOULD DEPOSIT ONE DECIGRAM OF RADIUM IN THE INTERNATIONAL BUREAU OF WEIGHTS AND MEASURES IN SÈVRES, FRANCE. IT CAN SERVE AS A SAMPLE.
HMM! THAT'S TRUE. I'LL HAVE TO REFINE MORE RADIUM . . . AND THAT TAKES WORK AND MONEY!

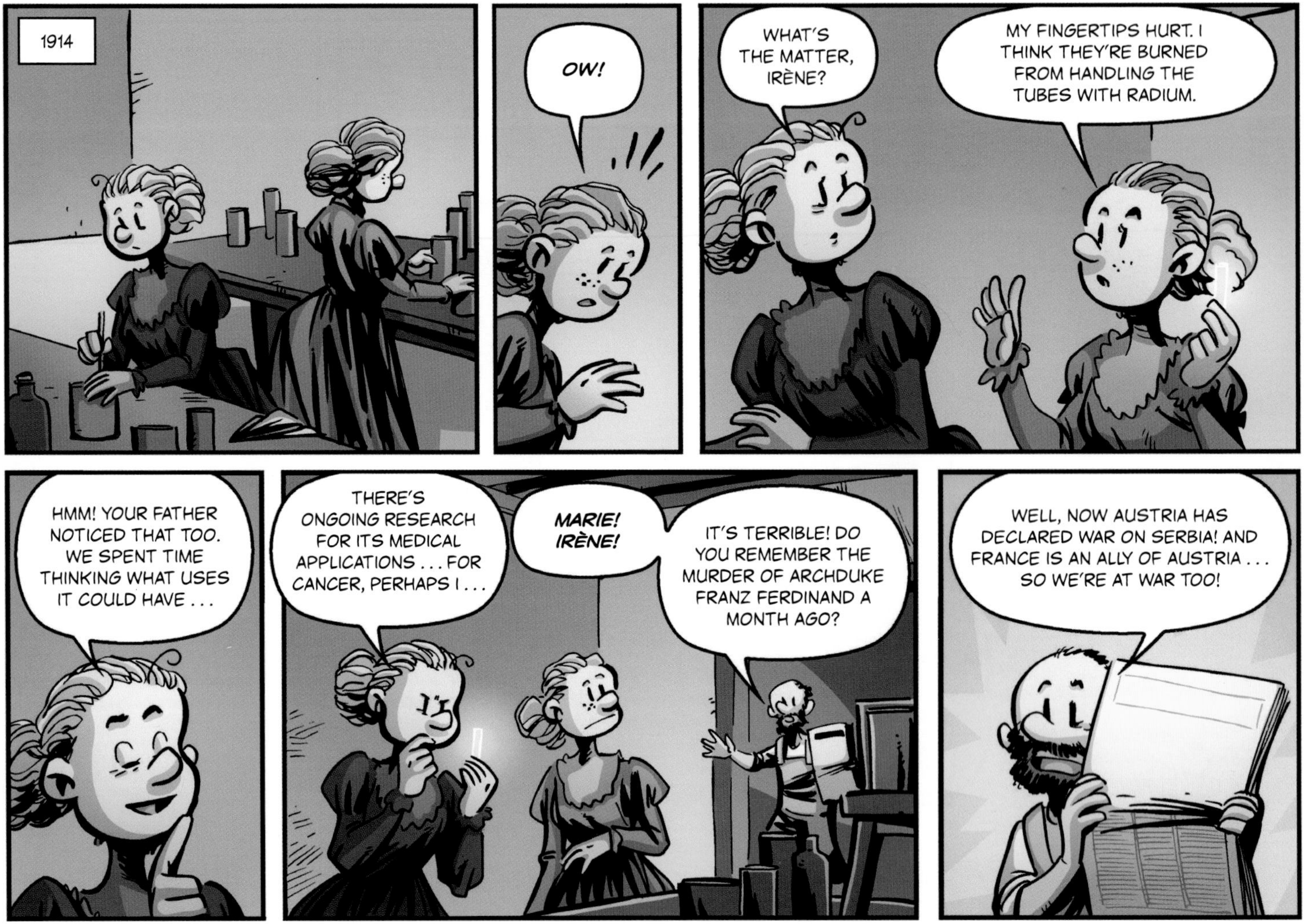

1914
OW!
WHAT'S THE MATTER, IRÈNE?
MY FINGERTIPS HURT. I THINK THEY'RE BURNED FROM HANDLING THE TUBES WITH RADIUM.
HMM! YOUR FATHER NOTICED THAT TOO. WE SPENT TIME THINKING WHAT USES IT COULD HAVE . . .
THERE'S ONGOING RESEARCH FOR ITS MEDICAL APPLICATIONS . . . FOR CANCER, PERHAPS I . . .
MARIE! IRÈNE!
IT'S TERRIBLE! DO YOU REMEMBER THE MURDER OF ARCHDUKE FRANZ FERDINAND A MONTH AGO?
WELL, NOW AUSTRIA HAS DECLARED WAR ON SERBIA! AND FRANCE IS AN ALLY OF AUSTRIA . . . SO WE'RE AT WAR TOO!

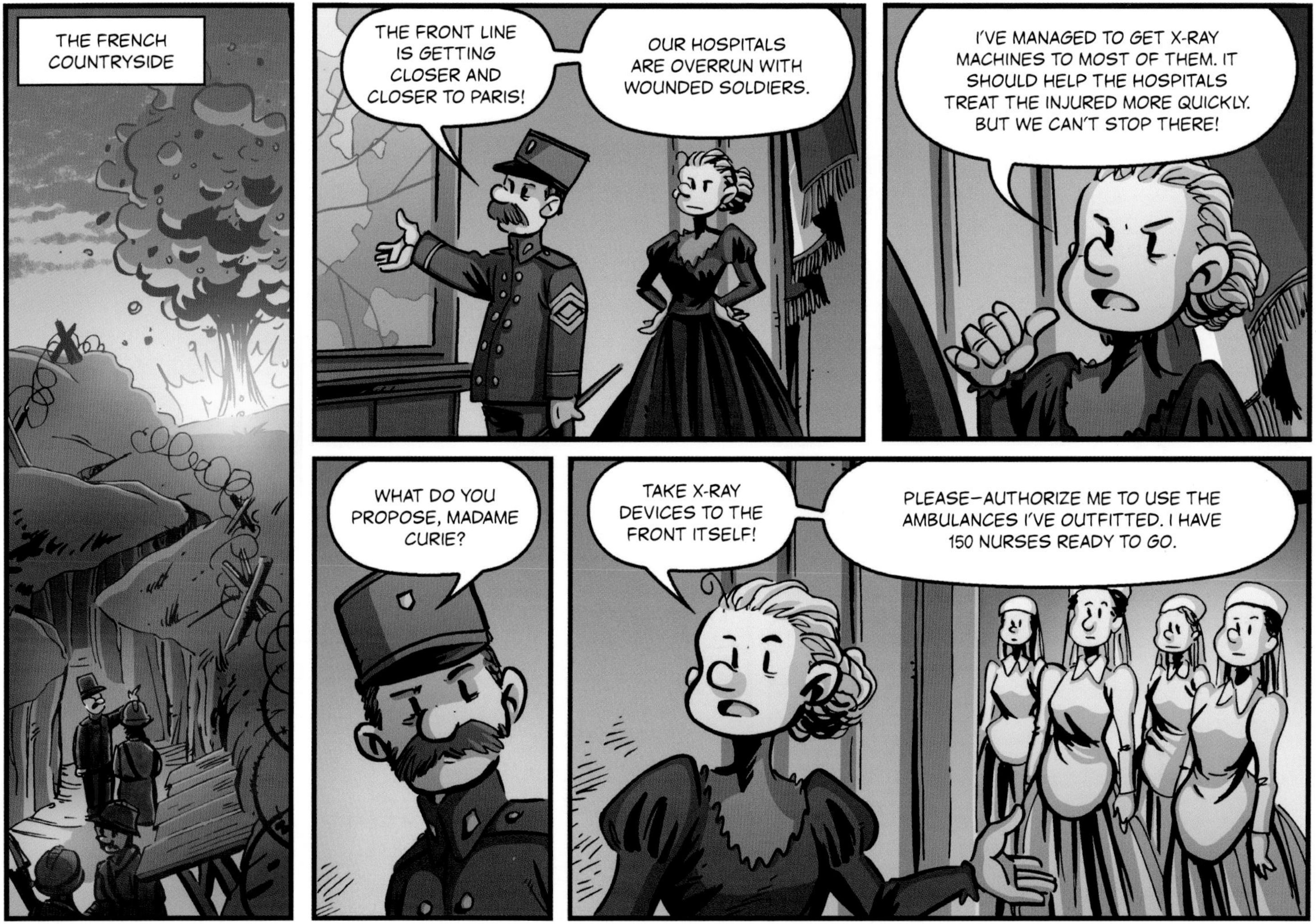
THE FRENCH COUNTRYSIDE
THE FRONT LINE IS GETTING CLOSER AND CLOSER TO PARIS!
OUR HOSPITALS ARE OVERRUN WITH WOUNDED SOLDIERS.
I'VE MANAGED TO GET X-RAY MACHINES TO MOST OF THEM. IT SHOULD HELP THE HOSPITALS TREAT THE INJURED MORE QUICKLY. BUT WE CAN'T STOP THERE!
WHAT DO YOU PROPOSE, MADAME CURIE?
TAKE X-RAY DEVICES TO THE FRONT ITSELF!
PLEASE—AUTHORIZE ME TO USE THE AMBULANCES I'VE OUTFITTED. I HAVE 150 NURSES READY TO GO.

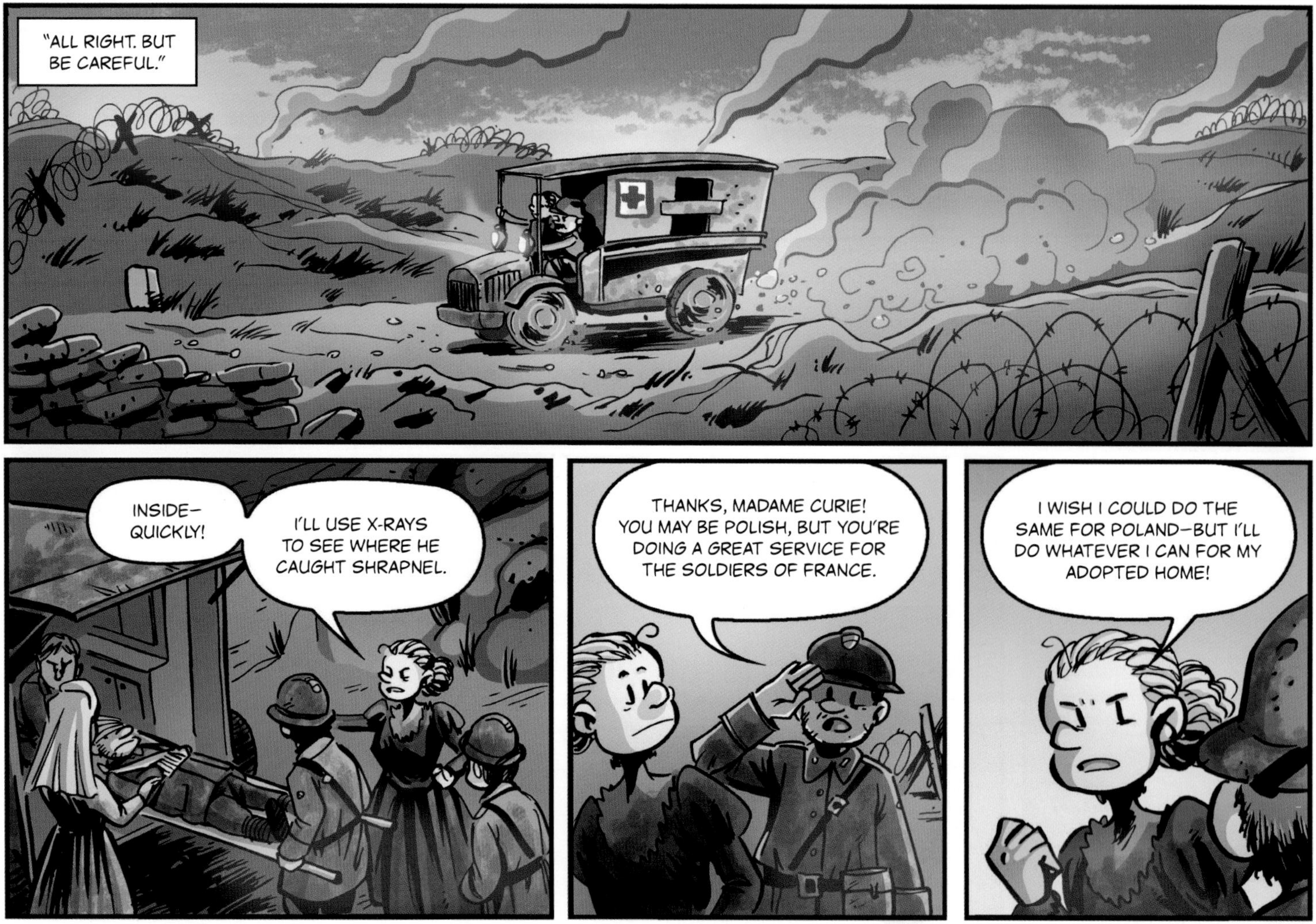
"ALL RIGHT. BUT BE CAREFUL."
INSIDE—QUICKLY!
I'LL USE X-RAYS TO SEE WHERE HE CAUGHT SHRAPNEL.
THANKS, MADAME CURIE! YOU MAY BE POLISH, BUT YOU'RE DOING A GREAT SERVICE FOR THE SOLDIERS OF FRANCE.
I WISH I COULD DO THE SAME FOR POLAND—BUT I'LL DO WHATEVER I CAN FOR MY ADOPTED HOME!

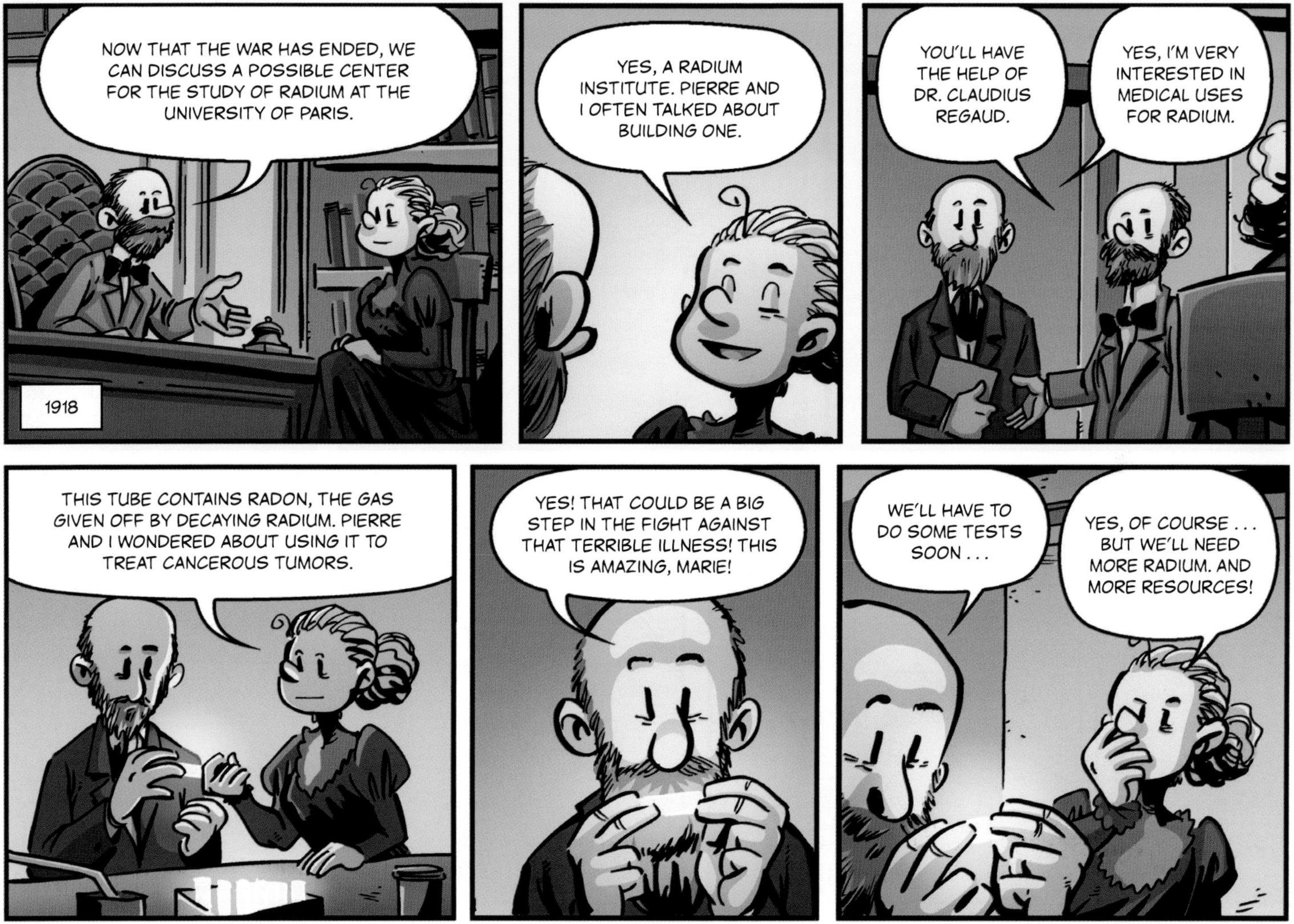
NOW THAT THE WAR HAS ENDED, WE CAN DISCUSS A POSSIBLE CENTER FOR THE STUDY OF RADIUM AT THE UNIVERSITY OF PARIS.
1918
YES, A RADIUM INSTITUTE. PIERRE AND I OFTEN TALKED ABOUT BUILDING ONE.
YOU'LL HAVE THE HELP OF DR. CLAUDIUS REGAUD.
YES, I'M VERY INTERESTED IN MEDICAL USES FOR RADIUM.
THIS TUBE CONTAINS RADON, THE GAS GIVEN OFF BY DECAYING RADIUM. PIERRE AND I WONDERED ABOUT USING IT TO TREAT CANCEROUS TUMORS.
YES! THAT COULD BE A BIG STEP IN THE FIGHT AGAINST THAT TERRIBLE ILLNESS! THIS IS AMAZING, MARIE!
WE'LL HAVE TO DO SOME TESTS SOON . . .
YES, OF COURSE . . . BUT WE'LL NEED MORE RADIUM. AND MORE RESOURCES!

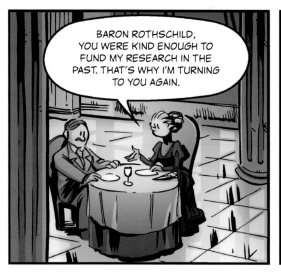

BARON ROTHSCHILD, YOU WERE KIND ENOUGH TO FUND MY RESEARCH IN THE PAST. THAT'S WHY I'M TURNING TO YOU AGAIN.

THE INSTITUTE WE'RE BUILDING WILL BE A HUB FOR RADIUM RESEARCH. THAT INCLUDES ITS ROLE IN MEDICAL TREATMENTS.

SAY NO MORE! PLEASE, BRING ME MY CHECKBOOK!

WE'VE SET UP A FOUNDATION TO TAKE CARE OF FUND-RAISING . . .

AND A FACTORY TO MAKE PRODUCTS FOR RADIOTHERAPY. THAT'S WHAT WE'RE CALLING THE MEDICAL USE OF RADIUM.

BUT THE MOST IMPORTANT THING IS THE INSTITUTE, WHERE WE CARRY OUT ALL OUR RESEARCH.

AT LAST, WE HAVE THE LAB PIERRE DREAMED OF!

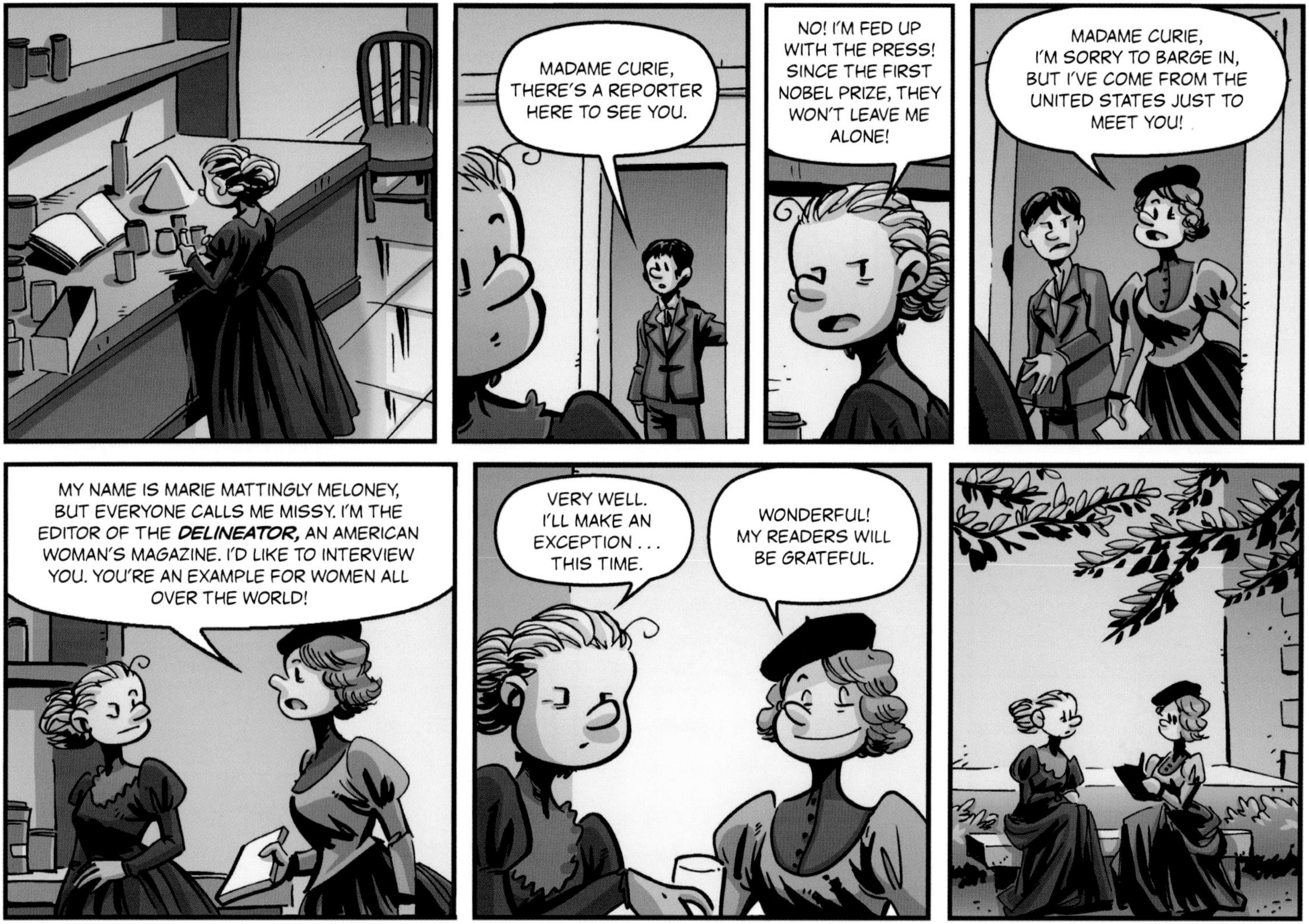
MADAME CURIE, THERE'S A REPORTER HERE TO SEE YOU.
NO! I'M FED UP WITH THE PRESS! SINCE THE FIRST NOBEL PRIZE, THEY WON'T LEAVE ME ALONE!
MADAME CURIE, I'M SORRY TO BARGE IN, BUT I'VE COME FROM THE UNITED STATES JUST TO MEET YOU!
MY NAME IS MARIE MATTINGLY MELONEY, BUT EVERYONE CALLS ME MISSY. I'M THE EDITOR OF THE ***DELINEATOR,*** AN AMERICAN WOMAN'S MAGAZINE. I'D LIKE TO INTERVIEW YOU. YOU'RE AN EXAMPLE FOR WOMEN ALL OVER THE WORLD!
VERY WELL. I'LL MAKE AN EXCEPTION . . . THIS TIME.
WONDERFUL! MY READERS WILL BE GRATEFUL.

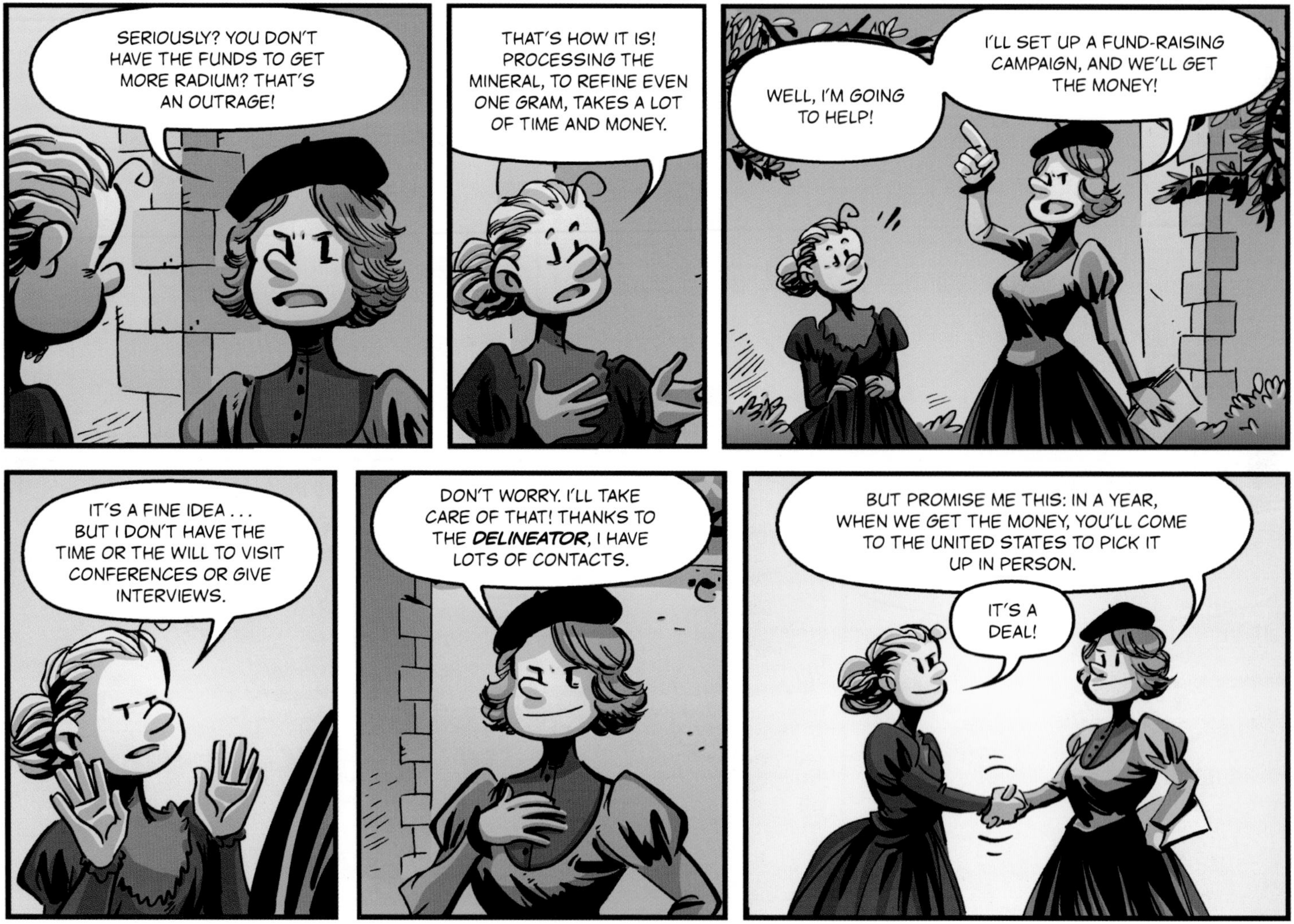
SERIOUSLY? YOU DON'T HAVE THE FUNDS TO GET MORE RADIUM? THAT'S AN OUTRAGE!
THAT'S HOW IT IS! PROCESSING THE MINERAL, TO REFINE EVEN ONE GRAM, TAKES A LOT OF TIME AND MONEY.
WELL, I'M GOING TO HELP!
I'LL SET UP A FUND-RAISING CAMPAIGN, AND WE'LL GET THE MONEY!
IT'S A FINE IDEA . . . BUT I DON'T HAVE THE TIME OR THE WILL TO VISIT CONFERENCES OR GIVE INTERVIEWS.
DON'T WORRY. I'LL TAKE CARE OF THAT! THANKS TO THE **DELINEATOR**, I HAVE LOTS OF CONTACTS.
BUT PROMISE ME THIS: IN A YEAR, WHEN WE GET THE MONEY, YOU'LL COME TO THE UNITED STATES TO PICK IT UP IN PERSON.
IT'S A DEAL!

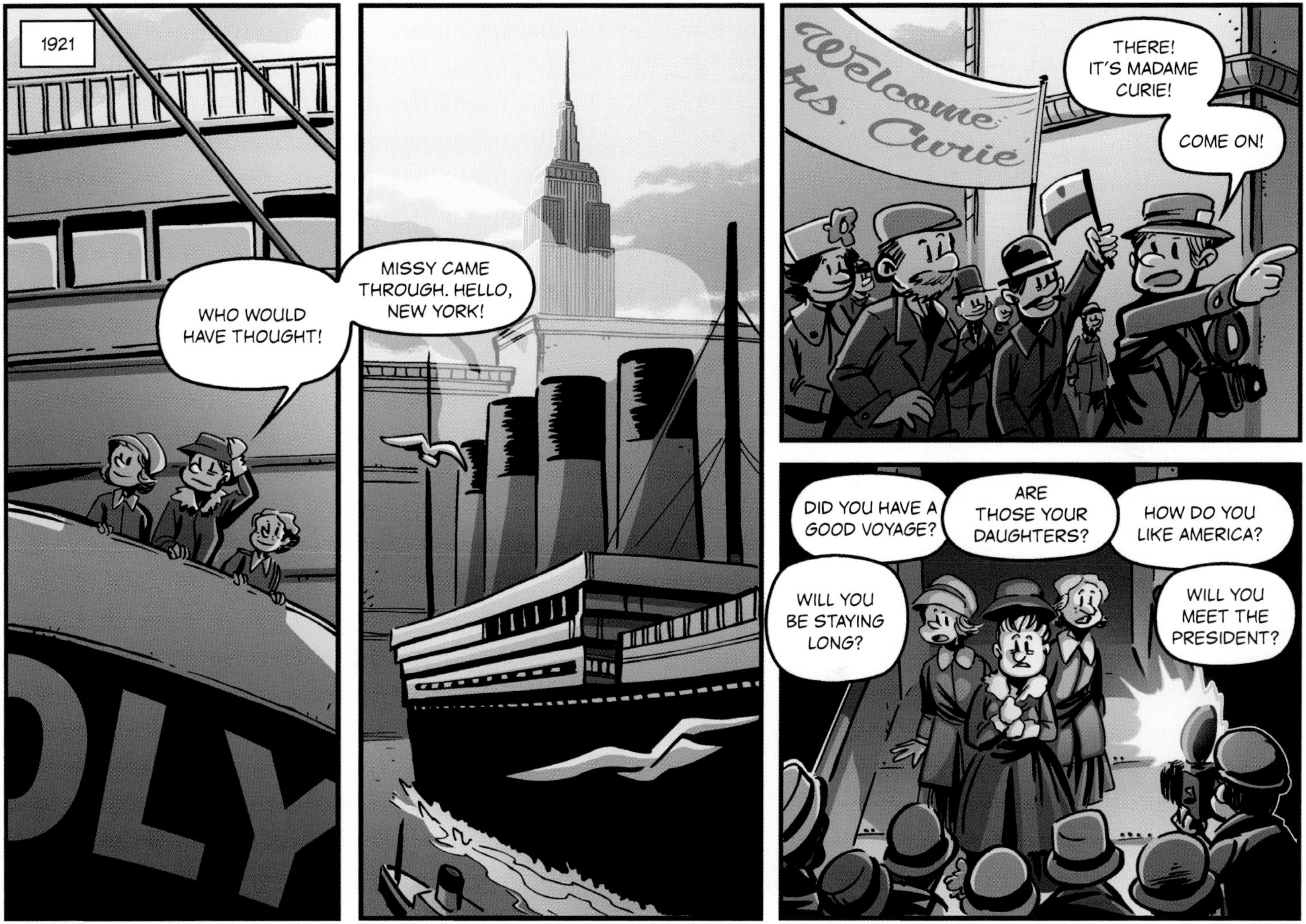
1921
WHO WOULD HAVE THOUGHT!
MISSY CAME THROUGH. HELLO, NEW YORK!
Welcome Mrs. Curie
THERE! IT'S MADAME CURIE!
COME ON!
DID YOU HAVE A GOOD VOYAGE?
ARE THOSE YOUR DAUGHTERS?
HOW DO YOU LIKE AMERICA?
WILL YOU BE STAYING LONG?
WILL YOU MEET THE PRESIDENT?

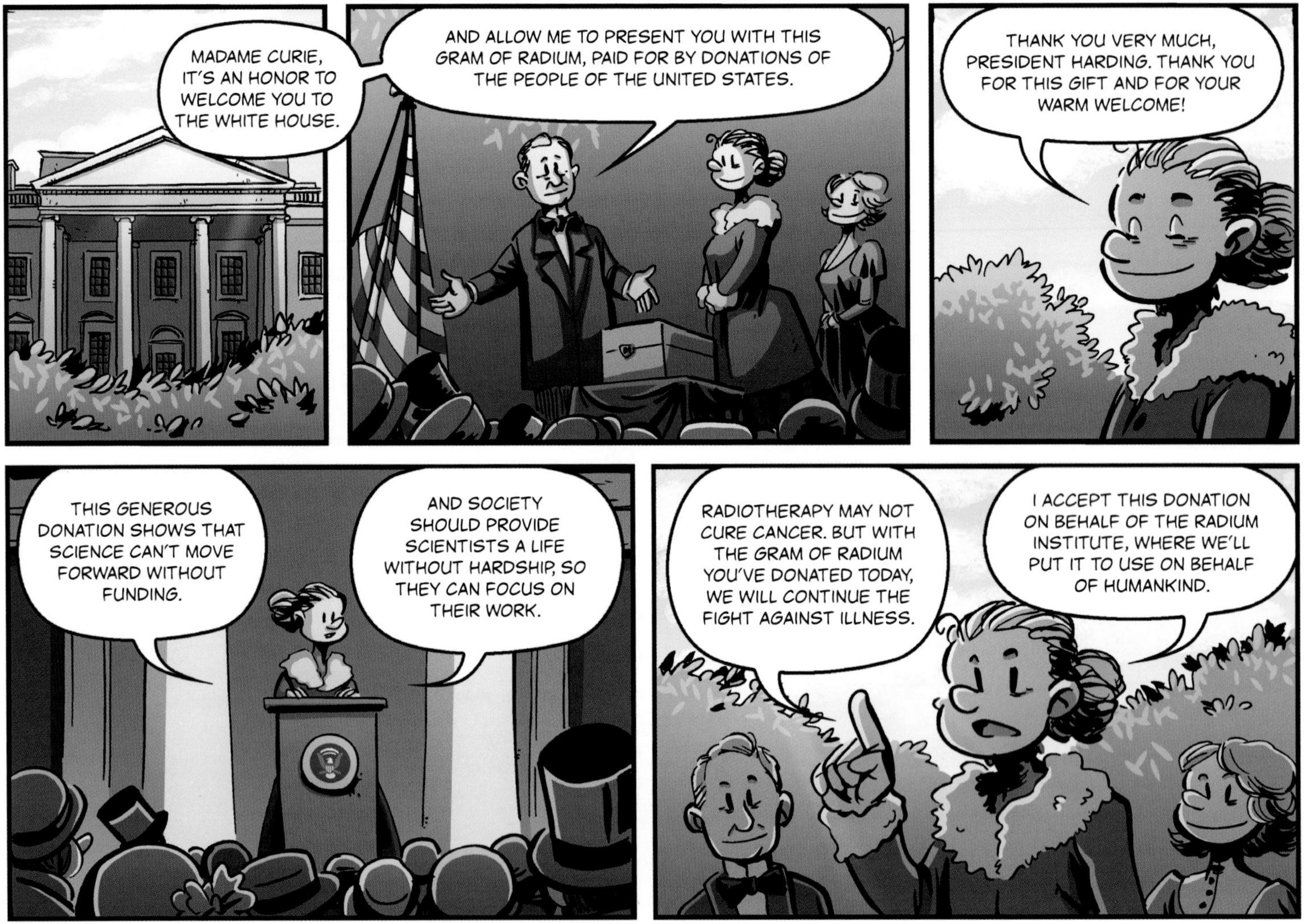
MADAME CURIE, IT'S AN HONOR TO WELCOME YOU TO THE WHITE HOUSE.
AND ALLOW ME TO PRESENT YOU WITH THIS GRAM OF RADIUM, PAID FOR BY DONATIONS OF THE PEOPLE OF THE UNITED STATES.
THANK YOU VERY MUCH, PRESIDENT HARDING. THANK YOU FOR THIS GIFT AND FOR YOUR WARM WELCOME!
THIS GENEROUS DONATION SHOWS THAT SCIENCE CAN'T MOVE FORWARD WITHOUT FUNDING.
AND SOCIETY SHOULD PROVIDE SCIENTISTS A LIFE WITHOUT HARDSHIP, SO THEY CAN FOCUS ON THEIR WORK.
RADIOTHERAPY MAY NOT CURE CANCER. BUT WITH THE GRAM OF RADIUM YOU'VE DONATED TODAY, WE WILL CONTINUE THE FIGHT AGAINST ILLNESS.
I ACCEPT THIS DONATION ON BEHALF OF THE RADIUM INSTITUTE, WHERE WE'LL PUT IT TO USE ON BEHALF OF HUMANKIND.

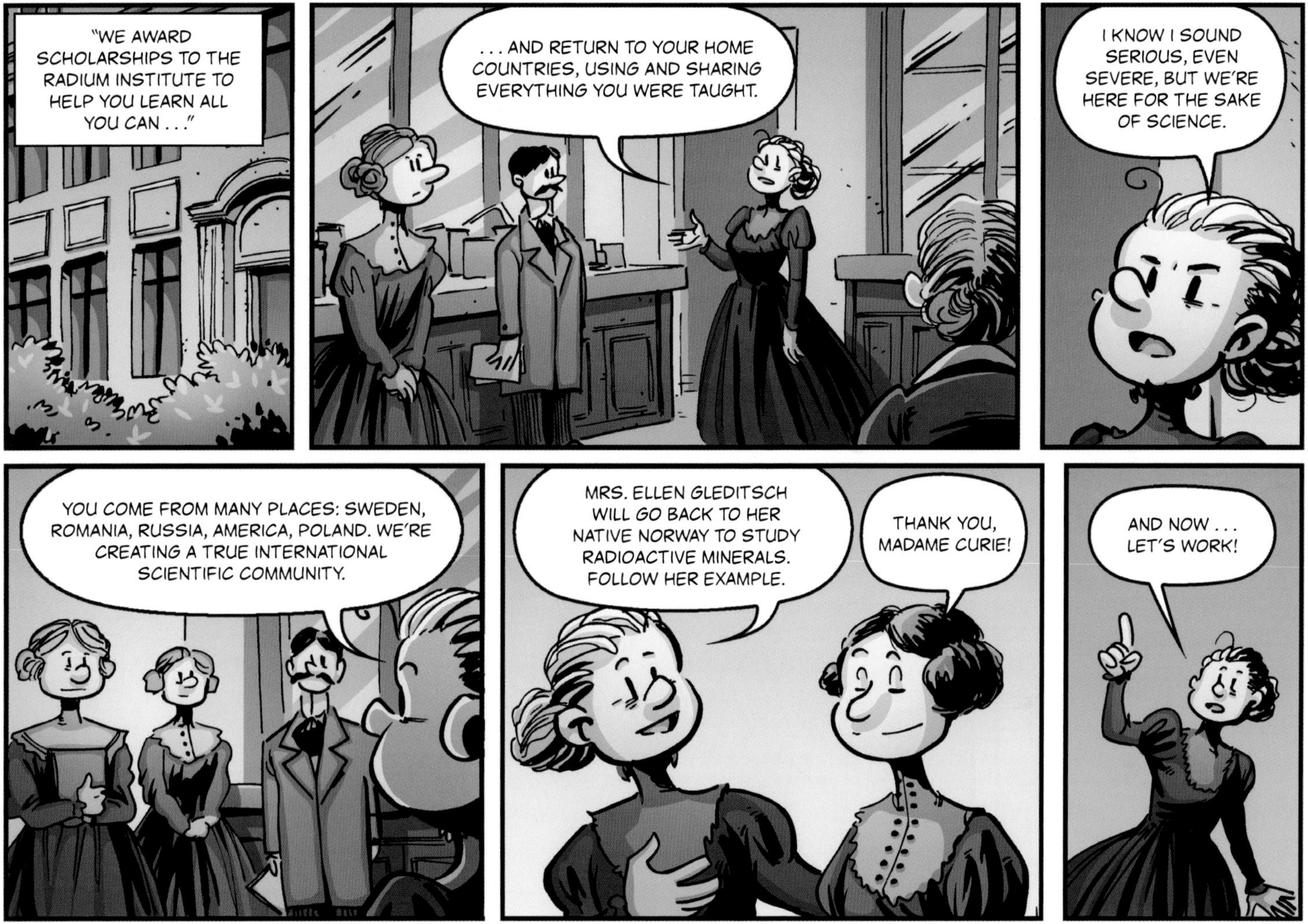
"WE AWARD SCHOLARSHIPS TO THE RADIUM INSTITUTE TO HELP YOU LEARN ALL YOU CAN . . ."
. . . AND RETURN TO YOUR HOME COUNTRIES, USING AND SHARING EVERYTHING YOU WERE TAUGHT.
I KNOW I SOUND SERIOUS, EVEN SEVERE, BUT WE'RE HERE FOR THE SAKE OF SCIENCE.
YOU COME FROM MANY PLACES: SWEDEN, ROMANIA, RUSSIA, AMERICA, POLAND. WE'RE CREATING A TRUE INTERNATIONAL SCIENTIFIC COMMUNITY.
MRS. ELLEN GLEDITSCH WILL GO BACK TO HER NATIVE NORWAY TO STUDY RADIOACTIVE MINERALS. FOLLOW HER EXAMPLE.
THANK YOU, MADAME CURIE!
AND NOW . . . LET'S WORK!

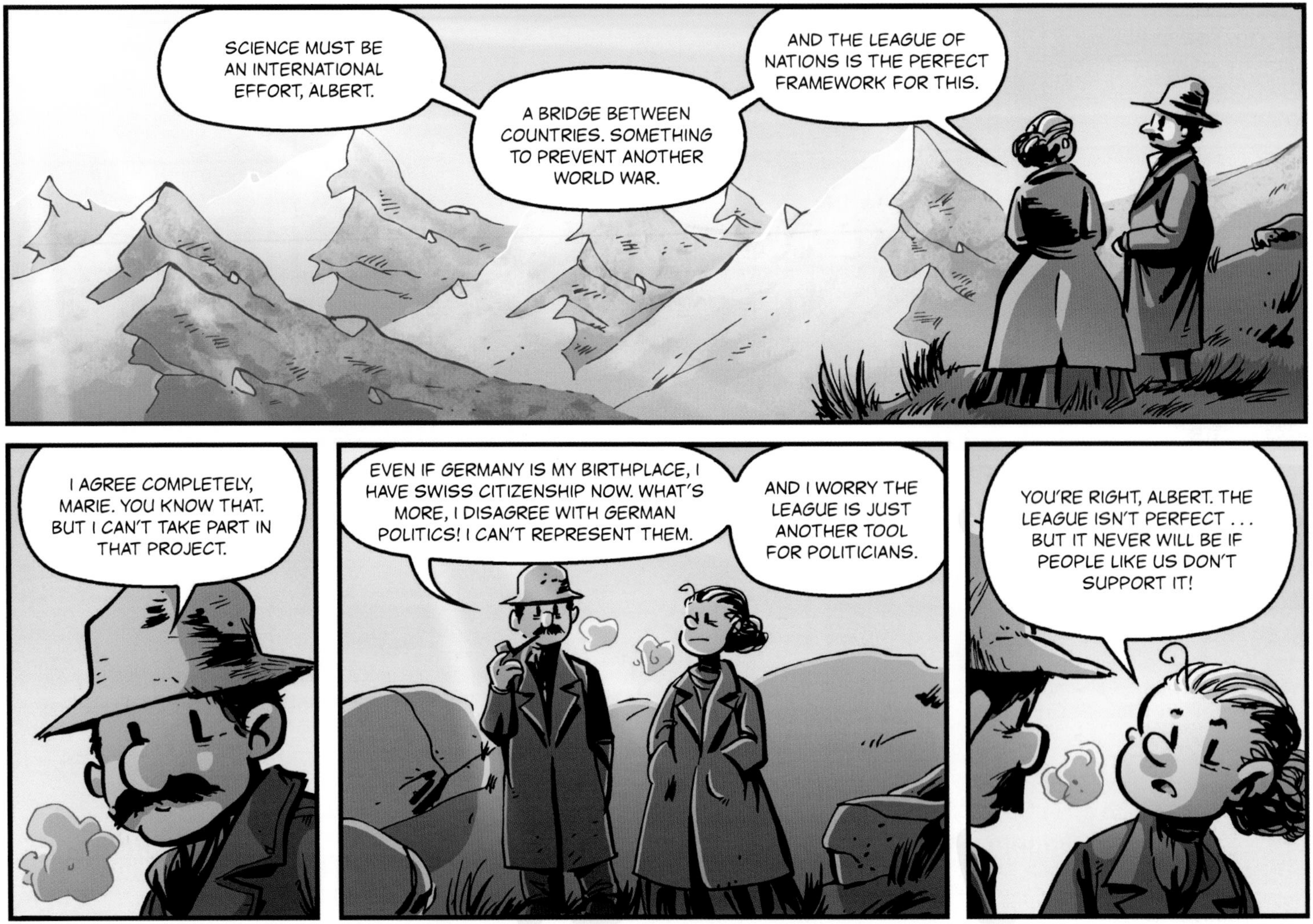
SCIENCE MUST BE AN INTERNATIONAL EFFORT, ALBERT.
A BRIDGE BETWEEN COUNTRIES. SOMETHING TO PREVENT ANOTHER WORLD WAR.
AND THE LEAGUE OF NATIONS IS THE PERFECT FRAMEWORK FOR THIS.
I AGREE COMPLETELY, MARIE. YOU KNOW THAT. BUT I CAN'T TAKE PART IN THAT PROJECT.
EVEN IF GERMANY IS MY BIRTHPLACE, I HAVE SWISS CITIZENSHIP NOW. WHAT'S MORE, I DISAGREE WITH GERMAN POLITICS! I CAN'T REPRESENT THEM.
AND I WORRY THE LEAGUE IS JUST ANOTHER TOOL FOR POLITICIANS.
YOU'RE RIGHT, ALBERT. THE LEAGUE ISN'T PERFECT . . . BUT IT NEVER WILL BE IF PEOPLE LIKE US DON'T SUPPORT IT!

NEW YORK CITY, 1929

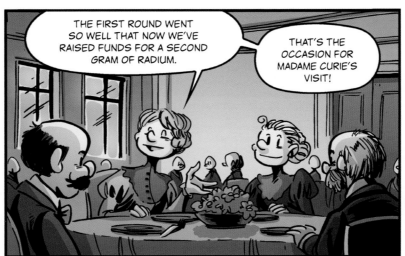

THE FIRST ROUND WENT SO WELL THAT NOW WE'VE RAISED FUNDS FOR A SECOND GRAM OF RADIUM.

THAT'S THE OCCASION FOR MADAME CURIE'S VISIT!

INDEED. I TOLD MISSY I WOULDN'T MAKE MANY PUBLIC APPEARANCES. I DON'T LIKE THEM.

BUT I HAD TO COME THIS EVENING, IN HONOR OF EDISON AND THE FIFTIETH ANNIVERSARY OF HIS INCANDESCENT LIGHT BULB!

ANNIVERSARY ...ESCENT LIGHT

YOUR FUND-RAISING FOR RESEARCH IN POLAND HAS GONE WELL TOO, HASN'T IT?

YES, MY SISTER BRONIA AND I HAVE RAISED MONEY IN EUROPE . . .

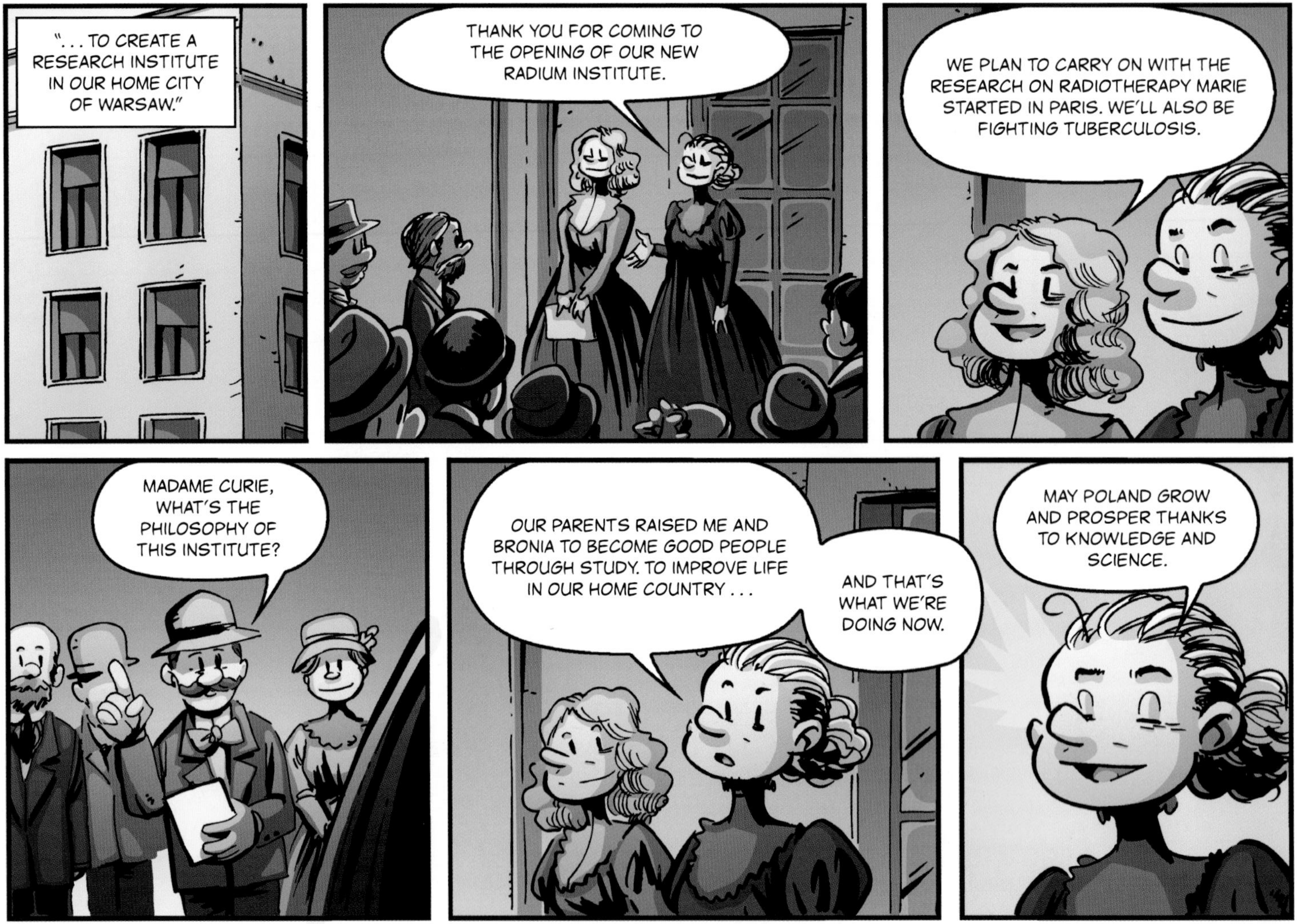
". . . TO CREATE A RESEARCH INSTITUTE IN OUR HOME CITY OF WARSAW."
THANK YOU FOR COMING TO THE OPENING OF OUR NEW RADIUM INSTITUTE.
WE PLAN TO CARRY ON WITH THE RESEARCH ON RADIOTHERAPY MARIE STARTED IN PARIS. WE'LL ALSO BE FIGHTING TUBERCULOSIS.
MADAME CURIE, WHAT'S THE PHILOSOPHY OF THIS INSTITUTE?
OUR PARENTS RAISED ME AND BRONIA TO BECOME GOOD PEOPLE THROUGH STUDY. TO IMPROVE LIFE IN OUR HOME COUNTRY . . .
AND THAT'S WHAT WE'RE DOING NOW.
MAY POLAND GROW AND PROSPER THANKS TO KNOWLEDGE AND SCIENCE.

TIMELINE

1867   Maria Salomea Skłodowska (often called Manya) is born in Warsaw, Poland, on November 7.

1873   Her father, Władysław Skłodowski, loses his position as a teacher in Russian-controlled Poland because of his pro-Polish views.

1891   Maria Skłodowska begins her studies at the University of Paris in Paris, France. She soon begins to use the name Marie.

1895   She marries Pierre Curie on July 26.

1898   Marie and Pierre Curie announce the discoveries of polonium in July and radium in December.

1903   Marie and Pierre Curie receive the Nobel Prize in Physics.

1906   Pierre Curie dies on April 19.

1911   Marie Curie wins the Nobel Prize in Chemistry.

1914   World War I begins.

1921   Curie tours the United States and receives a gram of radium from US president Warren G. Harding.

1934   She dies on July 4 from aplastic anemia.

GLOSSARY

CLANDESTINE: done in secret

ELECTRIC CHARGE: the amount of electricity held by a body, based on its balance of protons and electrons

ELECTROMETER: a device that measures electric charge

EMISSION: the act of sending out something such as energy or gas

FRONT: an area where military forces are fighting

GOVERNESS: a woman who is paid to care for and teach a child in the child's house

HYPOTHESIS: an unproven idea that leads to further study

MINERAL: a substance that is naturally formed under the ground

OCCUPIED: controlled by foreign soldiers or a foreign government

PITCHBLENDE: a mineral that contains radium and is the main ore-mineral source of uranium

QUANTUM PHYSICS: a branch of physics focused on very small particles

RADIOACTIVITY: having or producing a powerful form of energy called radiation

RAY: a thin beam of energy that moves as waves

RENOUNCE: to refuse or give up

SHRAPNEL: small pieces of metal that shoot outward from an exploding bomb, shell, or mine

SORBONNE: a public research university in Paris, France

THESIS: a long piece of writing that a researcher creates to earn a degree at a university

X-RAY: a powerful, invisible ray that can pass through various objects and make it possible to see inside some of them

FURTHER RESOURCES

Barr, Briony, Jeremy Barr, Gregory Crocetti, Ben Hutchings, and Ailsa Wild. *The Invisible War: A World War I Tale on Two Scales*. Minneapolis: Graphic Universe, 2019.

Bayarri, Jordi. *Albert Einstein and the Theory of Relativity*. Minneapolis: Graphic Universe, 2020.

Famous Scientists: Marie Curie
https://www.famousscientists.org/marie-curie

"The Genius of Marie Curie"
https://youtu.be/w6JFRi0Qm_s

Leigh, Anna. *30-Minute Chemistry Projects*. Minneapolis: Lerner Publications, 2019.

Marsico, Katie. *Key Discoveries in Physical Science*. Minneapolis: Lerner Publications, 2015.

INDEX